An Introduction to Teaching and Learning

Studies in Teaching and Learning
General Editor
Denis Lawton, B.A., Ph.D.
Professor of Education and Director,
University of London Institute of Education

In the series:

Denis Lawton *An Introduction to Teaching and Learning*
John Robertson *Effective Classroom Control*
Maurice Holt *Evaluating the Evaluators*
Richard Aldrich *An Introduction to the History of Education*
Edwin Cox *Problems and Possibilities for Religious Education*
Denis Lawton *Curriculum Studies and Educational Planning*
Rex Gibson *Structuralism and Education*
Richard Pring *Personal and Social Education in the Curriculum*
Malcolm Skilbeck (ed.) *Evaluating the Curriculum in the Eighties*
Keith Evans *The Development and Structure of the English School System*
I. A. Rodger and J. A. S. Richardson *Self-evaluation for Primary Schools*
Patrick D. Walsh *Values in Teaching and Learning*
Maggie Ing *Psychology, Teaching and Learning*

An Introduction to Teaching and Learning

Denis Lawton

HODDER AND STOUGHTON
LONDON SYDNEY AUCKLAND TORONTO

British Library Cataloguing in Publication Data

Lawton, Denis
An introduction to teaching and learning.
(studies in teaching and learning)
1. Education
I. Title II. Series
370 LB. 17

ISBN 0 340 26077 7 Paperback

First published 1981
Fifth impression 1986

Typeset by Graphic Consultants International Ltd, Singapore.

Printed and bound in Great Britain for
Hodder and Stoughton Educational,
a division of Hodder and Stoughton Ltd,
Mill Road, Dunton Green, Sevenoaks, Kent
by St Edmundsbury Press, Bury St Edmunds, Suffolk

Contents

Studies in Teaching and Learning

The purpose of this series of short books on education is to make available readable, up-to-date views on educational issues and controversies. Its aim will be to provide teachers and students (and perhaps parents and governors) with a series of books which will introduce those educational topics which any intelligent and professional educationist ought to be familiar with. One of the criticisms levelled against 'teacher-education' is that there is so little agreement about what ground should be covered in courses at various levels; one assumption behind this series of texts is that there is a common core of knowledge and skills that all teachers need to be aware of, and the series is designed to map out this territory.

Although the major intention of the series is to provide general coverage, each volume will consist of more than a review of the relevant literature; the individual authors will be encouraged to give their own personal interpretation of the field and the way it is developing.

Preface

A short book on a topic as vast as 'Teaching and Learning' cannot hope to answer all the questions or to provide 'answers' in any detail. But there is one major theme which runs through the whole of this text; it is that individual teachers and schools do matter! There is now evidence to support this view, some of which is included here. It is, therefore, important to clarify what it is about some teachers and some schools that makes them better than others.

In the 1940s and 1950s it was taken for granted that more spent on education would automatically result in improvement; conversely, deficiencies in education were seen largely as matters of under-provision – shortage of teachers, buildings or equipment. All that was needed was more money to put things right. During the 1960s this naive faith began to be shaken, and criticisms of various kinds became more common: hostile questions were asked about 'progressive' methods and curriculum development, concern was expressed about standards, and it was generally felt that education had failed to 'deliver the goods' – deliquency and vandalism were increasing rather than withering away, and pupils were still leaving school unable to read or do their sums. In the 1970s, the criticisms and feelings of dissatisfaction were sharpened into an accountability movement. At the same time, some critics even suggested that schools were positively harmful rather than just a waste of time.

It is understandable that teachers have been upset by these criticisms; at a time of falling rolls in schools their bargaining position is weak, and morale among teachers tends to be low. What is needed, however, is a positive response to the accountability movement in terms of increased professional awareness and better teaching methods. Teachers tend to see themselves as good practitioners rather than theorists, yet some kind of theory must underly their practice. I want to suggest that a good teacher needs not only to do the right things but to do them for the right reasons and to be aware of what he is doing. Only then can he counter criticisms of his practice, for questions about why new mathematics rather than traditional, or why mixed ability groups rather than streaming, can only be answered in *theoretical* terms. At the level of practice, most teachers are probably as competent as most solicitors or general practitioners (which perhaps does not say very much), but increasingly teachers will need to be able to explain and justify their practice.

This book will, therefore, be concentrating on a few major theoretical issues which are of great practical significance: for example, how certain traditions have developed in our educational system; why certain kinds of knowledge are regarded as more important than others; how to structure learning situations more effectively; as well as more fundamental questions about the nature of education and its purpose in a just society. Underlying these issues are even more fundamental questions about the nature of human beings and human life – are children naturally good or naturally evil? Is that a meaningful question? In a democratic society, can we continue within a tradition which is basically elitist? These questions are often seen as very remote from teaching the fourth form on Friday afternoon, but they are part of the reality which cannot be ignored.

London, 1981 Denis Lawton

1 The Social Context of Education

One of the distinctive features of the English education 'system' is that it does not fit neatly into normal classifications which make a sharp distinction between centralised and decentralised systems. The education system of English and Wales[1] operates on the basis of responsibility shared between central government, the local education authorities (LEAs) and the teaching profession. Official documents refer to education as a 'national system locally administered', with the Department of Education and Science (DES) a major partner rather than a central controller.

The reason for this shared responsibility is largely historical. State financing of education began with a modest grant of £20,000 for elementary schools in 1833, a time when government was viewed with even greater suspicion than it is now. State interference of any kind was frowned upon; government control of anything as serious as education was anathema to politicians and others brought up on the philosophy of *laissez faire* or non-intervention. As expenditure on education increased the government found it impossible not to get more involved, but throughout the nineteenth century there was continued opposition to the idea of government control of education. Successive education acts established a balance between the central authority and other interests. At first these other interests were mainly religious, later they became local and professional.

In 1870, W.E. Forster's Elementary Education Act maintained the principle that elementary schools should be mainly provided by the 'voluntary system' — that is, by religious bodies aided by state money — but since the intention was to 'cover the country with good schools', it was also necessary for the state to 'fill the gap', where no religious body made adequate provision.

School Boards, elected by local ratepayers, were established wherever necessary. These school boards were financed partly by central grants from the Education Department, partly by rates and partly by fees paid by parents. Church schools were financed in a similar way except that spending rates was explicitly forbidden for this purpose, and voluntary bodies were expected to raise money from their own church funds.

This dual system, apparently a very cumbersome British compromise, worked well in practice for many years. Sufficient schools were built to enable elementary education to become compulsory in 1880. In 1902, by the Balfour Act[2] secondary schools were included in the state provision, and by now, the division of control was not so much between central authority and religious (voluntary) bodies, as between central authority (the Board of Education) and local authorities.

By the beginning of the twentieth century teachers were beginning to emerge with claims for partnership, although at this stage very much a junior partnership. Elementary school teachers had begun to organise themselves as a professional body, or a trade union, in opposition to central control of the curriculum thirty years earlier. By 1862, expenditure on elementary schools was so great that many politicians became alarmed, and demanded both a reduction of expenditure and proof that taxpayers were getting value for money. The solution proposed by Robert Lowe[3] — the Revised Code of 1862 — prescribed a very narrow curriculum (reading, writing and arithmetic plus plain needlework for girls) and grant was paid to schools on the basis of the number of pupils reaching the 'standards' laid down by the Code. This system of 'payment by results' was hated by teachers, who in 1870 formed the National Union of Elementary Teachers. The word 'elementary' was omitted from the title after 1889 when the Union became the National Union of Teachers (NUT). From the very beginning the NUT was not only a political organisation but a highly effective body or pressure group representing the teaching profession. From the time of the first conference in 1870, the Union spoke on behalf of the profession, lobbied members of Parliament on educational issues, and from time to time put pressure on the Education Department. It carried on this tradition in later years with the Board, the Ministry and, eventually, the DES. On the specific question of 'payment by results' the Union was extremely vocal and by a process of constant agitation had succeeded by the end of the century in completely changing the system and abolishing 'payment by results'.

By the beginning of the twentieth century the NUT was beginning to share power with the central and local authorities. Other professional organisations also began to play a part: the Headmasters' Association was founded in 1890, the Assistant Mistresses (in Secondary Schools) became organised in 1884, and the Assistant Masters followed in 1891.

Throughout the 1920s and 1930s the NUT joined in the campaign for 'secondary education for all' which eventually resulted in the 1944 Act.[4] Meanwhile, in 1926 the regulations governing elementary schools had been abolished: all that remained was a *Handbook of Suggestions* for teachers (first produced in 1905) which stated that:

> ... the only uniformity of pratice that the Board of Education desires to see in the teaching of public elementary schools is that each teacher shall think for himself, and work out for himself such methods of teaching as may use his powers to the best advantage and be best suited to the particular needs and conditions of the school.

This was a remarkable change in attitude from the 1862 Revised Code 'payment by results'. Teachers were beginning to be regarded as professionals.. They felt, and many still feel, that they had won a victory against centralised bureaucracy and had gained a degree of professional autonomy that they would not lightly give up.[5]

1944 Education Act

The 1944 Act not only established free secondary education for all, but also transformed the education system in a number of other ways. The Board of Education became a Ministry, and LEAs were officially responsible for implementing the new education policy in three stages — primary, secondary and further. Secondary school regulations were superseded by the new Act so that secondary teachers as well as primary were now only given 'suggestions for consideration' rather than regulations to be observed.

Secondary teachers' professional autonomy was enhanced by two additional factors in the post-war period. Labour ministers of education after 1945 appeared to be very reluctant to take any part in curriculum control or even influence; one of them, George Tomlinson, made the famous statement that he 'knew nowt about curriculum'. In this policy they were probably reflecting the views of the civil servants in the Ministry of Education.

The second factor which tended to give increased power to the teachers was the fact that LEAs were so concerned with problems of reorganisation that they devoted little time to educational policy — in particular, matters of curriculum were very rarely discussed. Teachers were left to decide what to teach and how to teach it. The policy of secondary education for all meant that more buildings were required; many of the existing buildings were inadequate and badly equipped; and in addition to that, there was a desperate shortage of teachers. Organisation of buildings and provision of resources took priority over the discussion of curricular policy. Most LEAs, but not all, interpreted the Education Act as a recommendation for implementing a tripartite[6] system of secondary education. Before 1944, children went to elementary schools at the age five and most remained there until age fourteen. Some left at eleven and went to secondary schools either as fee payers or as scholarship winners. The post-1944 reorganisation meant that all pupils would now transfer to a secondary school at age eleven. But what kind of secondary school? The Act stated that LEAs had the responsibility for educating all children according to their ages, abilities and aptitudes. The pre-war Spens Report,[7] on the basis of very doubtful psychological evidence, had suggested that there were three kinds of children — academic, technical and those who were neither academic nor technical. These three kinds of children should have three different kinds of schools and three different kinds of curriculum. Most LEAs, therefore, adopted a system of grammar schools for about 20% of the age group, and secondary modern schools for the majority, with a tiny provision of places in technical schools. This became known as the tripartite system.

Selection

The alternative, favoured by London and a few other authorities, was to have comprehensive secondary schools for the whole ability range eleven to eighteen. This policy tended to be supported by the Left Wing of the teaching profession — the National Association of Labour Teachers — and perhaps a majority of the NUT. The question of a tripartite or a comprehensive secondary school system became the dominant debate in education from 1945 to 1980, and it is still not completely resolved. In the early post-war years, it could be said that LEAs were mainly concerned with buildings, secondary school teachers with organisation, and primary teachers and parents with the eleven-plus examination.[8] In those authorities with a tripartite or bipartite secondary system, it was necessary to *select* pupils completing their primary education either to go to grammar schools or secondary modern schools (and, in some cases, technical schools as well). Two problems arose out of the necessity to select at eleven plus. The first related to geographical differences in the percentage of grammar schools available for eleven-year-olds; the second concerned the lack of confidence in the selection procedure. It should perhaps be added that the official (Ministry of Education) attitude was that of 'parity of esteem': that is, that secondary grammar schools, secondary technical schools and secondary modern schools were different but equal; pupils must be allocated to schools according to their 'abilities and aptitudes', but a secondary modern school was in no way inferior to a grammar school. Parents and teachers, however, tended to see reality differently: those who were selected for grammar schools were 'successes' (they had passed the eleven plus); those who went to secondary modern schools were failures.

With the background of attitudes based on success and failure rather than neutral allocation, the eleven-plus selection process became a focus of attention and agitation. The geographical unfairness took many years to be revealed, but when it was made public it seemed to be a powerful argument in favour of abolishing the eleven-plus examination.[9] Essentially, the problem was that although the national figure of grammar school places was about 20%, each LEA was free to establish its own norm. Some LEAs provided grammar school places for more than 50% of pupils, others provided for fewer than 10%. Whether a child went to grammar school or not sometimes seemed to depend more on where he lived than his measured ability. It was difficult to justify such discrepancies as part of a national system, but given LEA autonomy, it would have been impossible for the central authority, the Ministry, to have imposed a national norm of, say, 20%.

The second difficulty concerned the validity of the selection procedures. Great publicity was frequently given to those 'eleven-plus failures' who managed eventually to succeed, gain admittances to university and get good degrees. Equally damaging were reports such as *Early Leaving*[10] (1954) which demonstrated that large numbers of pupils who had been selected for grammar schools did not make the most of their privileged opportunities, and left early or failed their examinations. This drew attention to the nature of the selection process. Once again, practices varied from one LEA to another, but a common pattern was to make use of standardised tests in English and arithmetic, together with an intelligence test. It was the use of intelligence tests which caused most controversy.

Intelligence tests had a very respectable history (see Chapter 3). In the 1920s and 1930s psychologists such as Godfrey Thomson had used intelligence tests to ensure that some clever working-class children got to grammar school rather than less intelligent middle-class children with clever teachers. An enormous amount of educational research had been carried out to improve the efficiency of the tests used. By the 1950s they were probably almost as good as they could be, but nevertheless they were far from perfect. Professor P.E. Vernon,[11] who has devoted a good ideal of his professional life to improving such tests, declared that about 5% of pupils were wrongly selected for grammar schools or modern schools. Others would have considered this to have been a very modest estimate, but even the figure of 5% when converted into actual human beings was a very large number. Much of the research seemed to fit in with common sense in stating that motivation appeared to be more important than a precise point on an IQ scale.

A Comprehensive System

Gradually, arguments in favour of a comprehensive system of some kind won the day not only among educationists but among parents and politicians. More and more LEAs reorganised secondary education along comprehensive lines. When the Labour Government in 1965 introduced a Circular (10/65)[12] requesting LEAs to draw up plans for a comprehensive system of reorganisation, most LEAs had already been convinced by the arguments. But these were arguments against the eleven-plus examination rather than arguments for comprehensive schools as an ideal. Underlying these practical difficulties of allocation were deep-rooted ideological differences in attitude to education and its purposes.

During the nineteenth century there had been two quite distinct traditions of education: public and endowed schools with high status knowledge and a curriculum based on the classics for the upper and upper middle classes; elementary schools with a very basic curriculum for the 'lower orders'. These two traditions had overlapped to some extent during the twentieth century, and the 1944 Education Act finally brought them together (apart from the independent schools themselves which remained outside this system to develop their tradition quite separately). What had happened prior to the 1944 Act was that the two nineteenth-century traditions which had been based on social class were giving way to a divided system based, supposedly, on intelligence or ability. The 1944 Education Act, as interpreted by those advocating a tripartite system, completed this stage of educational history. Grammar schools were to be places for educating an elite – not a social elite but an intellectual elite. It is probably true to say that for many people inside and outside education that attitude was acceptable so long as the intellectual elite would be selected fairly. Comprehensive schools, for them, became an attractive alternative only when it was demonstrated that eleven-plus selection was neither efficient nor fair, and that comprehensive schools might provide a convenient means of delaying selection – pupils could follow similar courses until thirteen or fourteen and then be selected. But there is a much more fundamental argument in favour of comprehensive schools which is sometimes referred to as the egalitarian view.

The egalitarian view of comprehensive schools rests on two main assumptions. The first is concerned with the purpose of education; the second with social justice. According to this view, a major purpose of education is to be a unifying social force – education should bind people together and produce harmony rather than divide them, socially or intellectually; education should, therefore, transmit a common culture by means of a common curriculum. Clearly, this could be achieved more effectively in one school rather than separate schools for, say, the academic and the less academic. The related 'social justice' argument is that if education is regarded as a benefit, then it should be made available to all rather than to just a few. To give a better education to some because they are intelligent is no more socially just than to give a privileged education to those with a big bank balance.[13]

For those advocating a social egalitarian view of the comprehensive school, the essential debate is about the content of the curriculum – what aspects of culture are so important that they must be transmitted to the next generation – rather than buildings and organisation. It has taken many years since 1944 for the debate about secondary education to reach that point: in the early post-war period, the major concern was whether to have comprehensive secondary schools or a tripartite system; in the 1960s and 1970s the debate turned to questions of school organisation — setting or streaming or mixed ability teaching. Only in the mid 1970s did curriculum become central, but the reason for this was less a general conversion to the common culture ideal than concern for standards, value for money and accountability. This brings us back once again to one of the central themes of this chapter – the control of education and in particular the control of the curriculum.

Curriculum Control and Planning

The golden age of teacher control was from 1944 to about 1960. As we have seen, during those years, neither the central authority nor the LEAs developed a policy on curriculum; this left teachers free to develop a tradition of professional autonomy on curriculum matters – the idea that curriculum is an expert business and only teachers should play any part in deciding on curriculum control and teaching methods. By 1960, however, there were signs that the period of harmony and consensus in education was coming to an end,[14] and there was also a growing suspicion that some voices within the central authority were urging more control over the school curriculum. In 1960, the Conservative Minister of Education, David Eccles, in a House of Commons debate on education, said that he regretted that parliamentary debates on this subject were usually devoted to bricks and mortar and matters of organisation rather the content of the curriculum. He announced his intention to 'make the

Ministry's voice heard rather more often and positively and no doubt controversially'. Eccles appeared to be particularly concerned that an important area of public concern, the curriculum, was closed to public scrutiny and discussion. Soon afterwards the Curriculum Study Group was established by the Minister. It never looked like the kind of body which would be a threat to teachers, or even LEAs, but the teachers' professional associations combined with the leaders of the LEAs and demanded the abolition of the Group. In 1963, the new Minister of Education, Sir Edward Boyle, said that the Curriculum Study Group would be replaced by a more acceptable body. The Lockwood Committee was set up and eventually recommended that there should be a Schools Council for the Curriculum and Examinations.[15]

The major difference between the Curriculum Study Group and the Schools Council was that the Council was not to be a creature of the central authority, but would be a neutral organisation in which teachers would have a majority membership on important committees. This could have been an opportunity for the teaching profession not only to gain control of the curriculum, but to develop a national policy for it. Unfortunately, however, this opportunity was missed. The main reason for this was that the tradition had by now grown up that the proper place for curriculum planning was inside schools. There was thus no place within the Schools Council for discussions about the *whole* curriculum, only for curriculum development in such a way that teachers could be assisted to improve their own curriculum planning and teaching method. In other words, the Council was committed to a policy of providing alternatives from which teachers would choose rather than developing a policy about the nature of the school curriculum. This 'cafeteria' approach has been a weakness. In time the initiative for curriculum planning was to pass away from teachers into the hands of the DES.

This tendency was assisted by the fact that throughout the 1960s and 1970s criticisms of education in general became more widespread. Criticisms were usually levelled at progressive methods and curriculum innovation, but they covered a wide range of dissatisfaction. It is also significant that the first of the Black Papers[16] appeared in 1969, taking a very traditional and conservative view of education.

The Department of Education and Science also appeared to be concerned about standards, and in 1974 set up the

Assessment of Performance Unit[17] to monitor standards in schools. In 1976, the new Permanent Secretary at the DES, James Hamilton, publicly criticised teachers for sheltering behind their expertise and appeared to be suggesting that the DES would be becoming more involved in curriculum planning.

The idea that teachers alone should not control the curriculum was not confined to the DES. There was also a growing consumer interest in education. Parents' organisations were becoming much more vocal. In 1976 the Taylor Committee,[18] which had been set up in order to examine the governing bodies of schools, received evidence which recommended that the curriculum was too important to be left to teachers and that reformed governing bodies should include parents, and that these governing bodies should exercise much greater control over the curriculum.

At the same time the DES was being pushed in the direction of greater concern over educational policy and curriculum planning. In 1976 the Tenth Report of the House of Commons Expenditure Committee focused attention on the lack of control that the DES seemed to have over how money was spent on education. The Expenditure Committee also criticised the fact that the teachers alone appeared to control the curriculum, and that the DES was not involved in any long-term planning of that kind. In October 1976 the Prime Minister, James Callaghan, also joined in the criticism of the teaching profession. In a speech at Ruskin College he put forward a view that schools should be more receptive to the needs of society and, in particular, the needs of industry. These also appeared to be a strong suggestion that schools were neglecting their function of providing sufficient training in the basic subjects.

The Labour Prime Minister's Ruskin College speech launched the 'Great Debate' on Education. A series of discussions were held throughout the country including questions about the control of the curriculum. The Great Debate led eventually to the production by the DES of a Green Paper *Education in Schools: A Consultative Document* (1977). In this document it was stated that the Secretary of State for Education could not abdicate from central responsibilities and the question was raised as to whether 'parts of the curriculum should be protected because there are aims common to all schools and pupils'.

The Green Paper was followed in November 1977 by a DES

Circular 14/77, which asked LEAs to conduct a review of existing curricular arrangements. So not only was the DES indicating that it still had a vital part to play in curriculum planning, it was also reminding LEAs of their responsibilities regarding curriculum. In this Circular it was clearly stated that the functioning of the education system in England and Wales depended on the effective co-operation of schools (i.e. teachers as well governors), LEAs, the DES and Her Majesty's Inspectors (HMI). It was stated that the Secretaries of State had no intention of changing that partnership but that they recognised the legitimate interest of others — parents, industry and commerce — in the work of the schools.

By 1979 the LEA survey had been completed and was reported by the DES.[19] This seemed to indicate that most LEAs were neglecting their curricular responsibilities and few had a satisfactory policy on curriculum planning. At the same time, HMIs had been carrying out a primary school survey and later a secondary school survey which seemed to indicate that curriculum planning at school level left much to be desired. In secondary schools, for example, far too much use was made of option systems and too little importance given to the idea of a common curriculum. This encouraged the DES to bring out (January 1980) a discussion document *A Framework for the School Curriculum*, which suggested that there should be a core of English, mathematics and science, which should be the basis of curriculum organisation within all schools. It was a very poorly argued document, but the content was of much less importance than the political intention behind it. The framework was clearly an indication, heralded in 1977 by the Green Paper, that the central authority wished to have much greater control of curriculum planning. The teaching profession had been given an opportunity to plan a national curriculum, but had not taken full advantage of it, thus leaving the DES with a good excuse to interfere.

Summary

This chapter has been concerned with four inter-related themes. First, the control of the education system. Second, the fact that England and Wales does not have a centralised system of education but a partnership between DES, LEAs and teachers. The partnership is not, however, a stable one — dominance patterns change as part of the changing social context. Third, underlying the question of control there are different ideologies of education. Total consensus about the purpose of education and its organisation is lacking. Fourth, these different ideologies have been particularly relevant in discussions of secondary school curriculum and organisation since 1944.

In the next chapter we shall take up the particular question of the values and ideologies underlying discussions about the school curriculum.

NOTES

1 **Most of the discussion** in this book will be confined to the educational system of England and Wales. Scotland and Northern Ireland have systems which are sufficiently different to justify separate treatment. Apart from the universities, which are included in the national provision, education in Scotland is the responsibility of the Secretary of State for Scotland; education in Northern Ireland is administered separately. Responsibility for Welsh schools is now part of the responsibility for the Secretary of State for Wales, but, unlike Scotland, the school in Wales can be considered as part of the same system as that of England. See Evans (1975) or Dent (1977) for the historical background.

2 **The Balfour Act (1902).** The 1902 Education Act was, unusually, piloted through the House of Commons by A.J.Balfour, the Prime Minister. Lord Londonderry, the President of the Board of Education, was in the House of Lords. The major author of the Act was Morant who became Permanent Secretary of the Board of Education from 1 November 1902. The 1902 Act was an attempt to cope with an increasing number of children in schools. The school leaving age had been raised to eleven in 1893 and twelve in 1899. Large numbers of pupils were also staying on in elementary schools beyond the compulsory age, some going on to 'higher grade' schools, or to 'higher tops' (in elementary schools). This kind of education was secondary education in all but name, but it had been declared to be illegal in 1899, a decision confirmed by a High Court judgment in 1900. This left the government with no alternative but to provide secondary education on a national scale. The Act empowered local education authorities to establish secondary schools, helped by grant and by direct capitation grant from the Board of Education. School boards were thus replaced by the new Local Education Authorities.

3 **Robert Lowe (1811-92)** was a Liberal politician who became

Vice-President of the Committee of Council on Education in 1859. In 1862 he introduced the Revised Code Regulations. The Code of 1862 set out the conditions on which grants were to be paid and stated specifically the contents of the elementary school curriculum. Before that date, grants had been made to teachers according to their qualifications, but from 1862, grants were paid to school managers, largely based on an annual examination of all children in the 'three Rs'. The pupils were in six stages or standards, the first to be taken by children of six years of age. This was the system of 'payment by results' which lasted almost until the end of the nineteenth century. The Code did not exclude the teaching of other subjects, but it nevertheless led to excessive concentration on the three Rs and to complaints by inspectors of mechanical teaching. Teachers were violently opposed to the Revised Code and so were many of Her Majesty's Inspectors (HMIs) including the best known of them, Matthew Arnold. Lowe has been treated very harshly by some historians, but he was simply carrying out with great efficiency the prevailing philosophy of his time, utilitarianism. His view was that the 1862 Revised Code would either be more efficient or would be cheap. In this he was correct, at least in the short run. The government grant fell by over 20% between 1862 and 1865. Attendance at school by the pupils rose at this time and despite the criticism of the narrow curriculum, children remained at school longer. However, the Code certainly led to a number of undesirable practices in schools: an emphasis on rote learning, partly to defeat the inspectors, and the cutting out of many more imaginative aspects of the curriculum. *See* Gordon and Lawton (1978).

4 **The Education Act 1944 (The Butler Act).** Much of the thinking and discussion behind the 1944 Act took place in the middle of the Second World War (1939-45). Mr R.A. Butler, President of the Board, issued a 'Green Book' in October 1941. This was a confidential document of proposals for reconstruction. After much discussion and general acceptance by both political parties, a revised version was published as a White Paper in 1943 (the White Paper on Educational Reconstruction). This formed the basis of a Bill which was presented to Parliament on 15 December 1943, and became law on 3 August 1944. Not only did the Board of Education become a Ministry, but the President of the Board was now a Minister with greater powers. The 1944 Act specified that local authorities required his approval for local schemes. Primary education was to begin at five, secondary by twelve, ending at fifteen and as soon as practicable, at sixteen. All fees were abolished. The Act is still the major piece of legislation governing education in England and Wales, and was a most important landmark.

5 **John White** (1975) suggests that the motive in giving greater freedom to teachers was not to promote professional autonomy, but to prevent the political control of the curriculum. In 1926, the Conservative President of the Board of Education, Lord Eustace Percy,

abolished the Elementary School Regulations. White suggests that there may have been similar thinking behind the lack of curricular prescription in the Butler Act of 1944. If this has any truth in it, then the civil servants in the 1940s and 1950s were carrying on with this traditional policy. It was also very much in accord with the nineteenth century view of non-intervention and the fear of government control of curriculum.

6 **The tripartite system of secondary education.** The idea of having three different kinds of secondary schools (grammar, modern and technical) became known as the tripartite system and was the centre of much educational debate and conflict. As in so many other educational matters in England, this system had antecedents a long way back. The Schools Inquiry (1864-8), often known as the Taunton Commission, recommended three grades of school depending on school leaving age (eighteen or nineteen, sixteen or seventeen, fourteen or fifteen) with quite different curricula. The Spens Report (1938) (see note 7 below) suggested that there were three types of children who needed three kinds of school and three kinds of curricula. This tradition was also preserved by the Norwood Report (1943). In practice, most LEAs gradually reduced the schools to only two types, secondary grammar, and secondary modern (secondary technical being incorporated in one or the other type of school or abandoned altogether). In effect, therefore, the tripartite system was a bipartite system.

7 **The Spens Report (1938)** suggested that there should be for three identifiably different types of children three kinds of secondary school called grammar, modern and technical. The theory was that parity of esteem should be maintained between all three kinds of schools – they should be different, but equal. It was also recommended that transfer from one type of school to another should be possible. The idea of dividing pupils into three categories of 'academic', 'technical' and 'practical' has since been completely discredited.

8 **Eleven-plus examination.** Strictly speaking there was no such thing as an eleven-plus examination – there was a selection procedure. Local Education Authorities had the responsibility for deciding which pupils would go to grammar, technical and modern schools. They normally used standardised tests to pick out the academic, the technical and the others. The tests used were usually an intelligence test, together with standardised ability tests in English and arithematic. Primary school teachers saw this process as a question of preparing their pupils to do well on the tests. Very soon the process became known as the 'eleven-plus test' or the 'eleven-plus examination'. The policy of parity of esteem, or regarding the three types of school as different but equal in prestige, soon broke down: partly because teachers and parents regarded the selection procedure as a pass or fail test; partly because the products of grammar schools as compared with the products of secondary modern schools were accorded higher status

by society – thus it was impossible to avoid the schools themselves having a different status. Olive Banks (1955) has written a most interesting book about this question.

9 **Abolishing the eleven-plus examination.** Professor Brian Simon in an address to the Annual Conference of the Confederation for the Advancement of State Education in 1965 gave a most graphic example of the unfairness of the selection system:

It is now clear that the main inequalities in British education today (i.e. 1965) are due to three factors: difference in social class, in sex, and in geographical location.

If you happen to have had the luck to have been born a boy in Cardiganshire, your father in the professional or managerial class, your chance of achieving full-time higher education would almost certainly be about 80% — that is, of every ten children in this class, eight would achieve higher education. If, on the other hand, you were born as the daughter of a semi-skilled or unskilled worker living in West Ham, your chance of reaching full-time higher education would probably have been less than 0.5%. I say 'probably', because these figures are not based on a survey of the actual situation in these two areas as far as class and sex differences and opportunity are concerned; the assumption I have made is the not unreasonable one that these differences are the same in these two areas, as they are in the country as a whole.

These figures quantify the extent of differences in opportunity at their extremest points; they show that the Cardiganshire middle-class boy has roughly one hundred and sixty times as much chance of reaching full-time higher education than the West Ham working class girl; and this when a country has, in a formal sense, committed itself to a policy of equality of opportunity.

The full adress has been reprinted in a book by Brian Simon (1971).

10 **Early Leaving Report (1954).** The Early Leaving Report was a report of the Central Advisory Council for Education (CACE) issued in 1954. The Council had been given the task of looking at the factors influencing the age at which boys and girls leave secondary schools and the desirability of increasing the proportion staying on until eighteen. In its Report, the Committee saw the problem as partly a question of home background (mainly social class). They also realised that there were difficulties in the selection procedure. They saw the problem as a choice between grammar schools either taking a larger number of pupils and wasting public money, or taking fewer pupils and wasting talent. The Report is of considerable historical interest since it attempted to apply sociological methods to this particular educational problem. It is also of historical interest since it was still not totally committed to the egalitarian principles officially enshrined in the 1944 Education Act. The major concern was with wastage of places rather than equality of opportunity.

11 **Professor P. E. Vernon.** Professor Vernon spent much of his career at the University of London Institute of Education, and was responsible for a good deal of research into tests and testing. In 1957, he edited an Enquiry by the British Psychological Society, *Secondary School Selection,* which was extremely critical of the use being made of tests although expressing a basic satisfaction with the tests themselves. Later Professor Vernon became interested in the cross-cultural differences in intelligence and came to the conclusion that what we refer to as intelligence or IQ is very much a Western European middle-class skill which is partly innate, but partly learned.

12 **DES Circular 10/65.** In 1965, Anthony Crosland was Secretary of State for Education; he issued a circular to Local Education Authorities requesting them to draw up plans for a comprehensive system of reorganisation. This was his attempt to put economic pressure on those LEAs which were delaying the official policy of reorganising secondary education on comprehensive lines. It was a politically significant circular since it represented an attempt by central government to enforce its political will on local authorities with different views about how education should be organised. It was only successful up to a very limited point since a few local authorities continued to carry out delaying tactics throughout the 1960s and 1970s.

13 **Social justice.** Throughout the 1930s and 1940s, the view of many reformers in education was that opportunity should be provided for intelligent working class (and other) children who could not afford fees in secondary education. For this group of educationists or politicians the 1944 Education Act was interpreted in the tripartite way as secondary education for all, but a better education for the intelligent. This may be a misrepresentation of the desires of those reformers, who expressed the wish to have parity of prestige, but in effect, that is what happened. More money was spent per pupil in grammar schools than in secondary modern schools. But even if the same amount of money was spent there are others of a more egalitarian bent who would regard the tripartite system as unjust. They would argue that simply putting children into different schools will automatically result in some being treated as superior and others as inferior. This is not to suggest that all pupils of a given age have exactly the same kind of education, but simply that methods must be devised so that the less intelligent get just as good an education as those who are more intelligent. This does not mean that they will reach equal standards of achievement, but that they should have equality of access to important kinds of knowledge. This point will be more fully developed in later chapters in this book.

14 **Professor Maurice Kogan** has written about this end of consensus in a number of publications including *The Politics of Educational Change* (1978).

15 **The Schools Council.** Since 1964 the Schools Council has been responsible for most of the curriculum development and research in England and Wales. In 1963, Sir Edward Boyle, the Minister of Education, set up a working party under Sir John Lockwood. The Lockwood Report suggested the establishment of a body under the title *The Schools Council for the Curriculum and Examinations*. The Report also recommended that the Council should take over the functions of the Secondary Schools Examinations Council from September 1964. The Council has been responsible for a large number of publications, but by the mid 1970s the Schools Council was being increasingly criticised. Its constitution was reviewed in 1977 giving much less power to the teaching profession.

16 **The Black Papers.** These were an influential series of papers about various aspects and levels of education from primary school to university. They were edited by C.B.Cox and A. E. Dyson and were originally published by the Critical Quarterly Society. The first was *Fight for Education* (1969). The papers varied enormously in quality. Perhaps the best paper of all was that of Bantock on 'Discovery methods' (1969). They should be seen as the symptom rather than the cause of the reaction against progressive education in the 1960s and 1970s.

17 **The Assessment of Performance Unit (APU).** The beginning of the APU was announced in August 1974 in the White Paper *Educational Disadvantage and the Educational Needs of Immigrants* (Cmnd 5720). This White Paper was the response by the DES to the Report on Education by a House of Commons Select Committee on Race Relations and Immigration. In 1974 and 1975 the APU was presented as a means of testing disadvantaged children in order to diagnose their special difficulties. In successive years, however, less and less emphasis has been placed on the needs of the disadvantaged and more and more on monitoring standards. Apart from this political difficulty, there are also theoretical problems associated with item-banking and the Rasch model. *See* Lawton (1980).

18 **A New Partnership for our Schools,** usually referred to as the Taylor Report, (1977).

The Taylor Committee was set up by the Secretary of State for Education, Reginald Prentice, in April 1975, to examine governing bodies of schools. The Committee reported in 1977 and recommended additional powers for school governors. The Report has not been accepted in its entirety, but some provisions were incorporated into the 1980 Education Act. The existence of the Committee provided many pressure groups with an opportunity to make their views known not only about governing bodies of schools, but also about the general management of schools and the content of the curriculum. It was during this time that some voices were heard to say that the curriculum was too important to be left to teachers.

19 **The 1977 Green Paper** on Education *(Education in Schools: A Consultative Document)* required LEAs to undertake a survey of curricula in the schools in their authority. Details of these requirements were included in Circular 14/77 'Local Education Authority Arrangements for the School Curriculum' (DES 1977). When the results of this survey were published in December 1979, it was clear that some authorities had far too little knowledge and far too little control over the curriculum for which they were legally responsible. The full title of this Report is 'Local Authority Arrangements for the School Curriculum: Report on the Circular 14/77 Review'.

2 The Curriculum

In Chapter 1, it was implied that the control of the curriculum is a key feature of any educational system. In England, teachers have, theoretically, a good deal of control; but this has recently been subject to debate and criticism. A related problem is the content and organisation of the curriculum. This is often taken for granted by teachers and pupils: teachers see it as their job to teach the curriculum; pupils as theirs to learn certain packages of knowledge; neither party is expected to ask 'why?'

In recent years, however, the curriculum has been subject to scrutiny, debate and criticism.[1] Two very different kinds of attack are made: first, that the curriculum is old-fashioned or has failed to keep up with social change; second, that schools devote too much time to 'frills' and modern approaches but neglect the basics.

Holding one or other of those views is likely to be related to basic values which determine attitudes to education in general and to the curriculum in particular. The purpose of education can be seen at one extreme as a means of developing individuals to enjoy the best that life has to offer; or, at the other extreme, as a means of socialising or conditioning the young into conformity — becoming good citizens and useful, obedient workers. The first view night encourage a wide, comprehensive[2] curriculum; the second, a narrow basic programme probably with a stress on rote learning and preparation for work.

For some social and educational theorists, human beings are essentially evil: for those who hold this view, the major purpose of education is to stamp out greed, cruelty, selfishness and laziness, and to instill qualities such as obedience, kindness, co-operation with others and hard work. Another group of social and educational theorists claims that children are essentially good and naturally virtuous, but they may be corrupted by an imperfect society. For this group of theorists, the purpose of education is to allow children to develop 'naturally', to try to protect them from the evils of society, and to avoid their being corrupted.

The view that human beings are naturally selfish has a long history. The seventeenth-century English philosopher, Hobbes, made this assumption and based his social and political theory upon it. Durkheim, the nineteenth-century French sociologist and educationist, followed in the same tradition. On the other hand, many of the so-called 'progressive'[3] educational and social theorists such as Rousseau, Froebel, and more recently, A.S. Neill and John Holt have assumed children's innate goodness.

If children are 'naturally evil', which was the dominant view in the nineteenth century, then there are many educational consequences. Obedience will be much more important than giving children freedom to develop their own individuality; children will be expected to sit still in their desks and carry out carefully and methodically the instructions given to them by their strict teachers. The major purpose of education will be to mould the child into what are regarded as socially acceptable habits and necessary knowledge. Once the educational programme gets beyond the basic skills and habits the content of the curriculum will stress traditional subjects and disciplines rather than self-expression. Learning by rote will feature as an important method of acquiring knowledge. Questioning will be discouraged. There are many descriptions of this kind of school, and this kind of view of the purpose of education in nineteenth-century novels, especially those of Charles Dickens. Those Victorians who practised this kind of educational programme were not necessarily cruel individuals; they were simply reflecting the dominant social philosophy of that age. Most adults really believed that children had to be disciplined for any signs of wickedness and trained to obey authority: without such harsh treatment of children it was believed that they would grow up as selfish, destructive individuals, and civilisation would completely disappear.

There have always been some who opposed this view, of course. In the eighteenth century Rousseau, in rejecting this view, suggested that the social tranquillity achieved by the social philosophy of Hobbes would resemble the peace and quiet of a dungeon. Rousseau also rejected the notion of 'original sin' and went to the other extreme in saying that 'the first impulses of nature are always right'. Rousseau is also important for refusing to see children as adults on a small scale. He insisted that we should look upon children as individual human beings passing through stages of development which are important in their own right. For him, therefore, it was quite wrong to see education as a preparation for adult life – childhood was important in its own right and children should be allowed to develop without too much interference from the adult world. 'Nature would have them children before they are men. If we try to invert this order we shall produce a forced fruit immature and flavourless.' Rousseau's views have, in many respects, dominated 'progressive' education ever since.

It would be a mistake to think that either of these two models, the naturally evil or the naturally good, exists in a pure form, apart from a very small minority of practitioners, but it is certainly true that the climate of social and educational opinion changes from time to time and place to place. In nineteenth-century England, the original sin view was certainly dominant, whereas by the middle of the twentieth century many teachers, especially primary school teachers, had been given a version of the 'child-centred' educational model.

The child-centred curriculum was enshrined in the 1967 Plowden[4] Report in which even the title *Children and their Primary Schools* proclaims the underlying philosophy. In this report, which was extremely influential in the late 1960s and early 1970s, children are portrayed as naturally curious, able to make discoveries for themselves, and having a natural ability to choose activities which will give them educational knowledge and experience. The role of the teacher, according to the Plowden Report, was to be a facilitator of learning. He should not instruct children or provide them with too much ready-made knowledge; his task is to provide opportunities for pupils to discover and create knowledge for themselves, to be creative and to grow socially, emotionally, intellectually, physically, morally and spiritually.

That is probably a fair description of the dominant child-centred view of education and the curriculum. It is dominant in the sense that most primary school teachers have had that view given to them as part of their official training; and it is the view reflected in official reports and most textbooks on primary education. Despite that, recent surveys[5] would seem to indicate that only a minority of teachers actually practise according to these progressive methods.

There are two other, fairly popular, views of curriculum which are much more in the 'natural evil' tradition than the child-centred. The first of these is the knowledge-centred view of curriculum; the second is the society-centred view.

The knowledge-centred view of curriculum is much more associated with secondary schools than primary schools; and with the grammar school tradition rather than the secondary modern school tradition. The knowledge-centred view assumes that the major purpose of education is to pass on the knowledge gained by previous generations to the next generation, and that this is most appropriately done in packages referred to as subjects. This view is reflected in the training of teachers in England where most secondary school teachers are specialists in only one subject and are trained only to teach that specialism. There is, of course, some truth in this view. All children do need to acquire certain kinds of knowledge. But the knowledge-centred approach cloaks a number of imperfections in the traditional secondary school curriculum. There are, for example, a number of important kinds of knowledge which are simply not represented on the typical secondary school timetable (for example, political understanding). Another failure of the knowledge-centred curriculum is that by compartmentalising knowledge into discrete subjects a good deal of co-operation between those subject areas is missed, as well the practical application of knowledge (for example, the recent Secondary School Survey[6] conducted by HMI showed that pupils in secondary schools were competent at certain kinds of mathematical skills in mathematics lessons, but could not apply their knowledge either in other lessons or in practical situations). The present subject-dominated secondary curriculum must at least be scrutinised and criticised rather than taken for granted.

Finally, there is the 'needs of society' or society-centred curriculum. It is often suggested that the curriculum should be planned according to the changing nature of our society, and in particular, the fact that we are an industrialised and commercial society. A recent example of this approach was the speech by James Callaghan, at Ruskin College, Oxford, in 1976, when he was Prime Minister, launching the 'Great Debate' on Education. According to this view, or perhaps a crude version of it, the main purpose of education is to prepare the young for adult society, especially for their work-role in industrialised society. Schools should, therefore, have careful regard for the needs of industry and should plan the curriculum accordingly. Even reasonably sophisticated educationists sometimes fall into the trap of suggesting that because Britain is now part of the European Economic Community all children should spend much more time learning foreign languages. Similarly, industrialists often demand that schools should concentrate much more attention on science and mathematics, and go on to specify the kind of science and mathematics which 'industry needs'. It would be quite wrong to dismiss these arguments completely, but they do break down if they are employed as the only justification for the curriculum.

There are two major fallacies involved in this approach to the curriculum. First, teachers should not be assumed to have an automatic duty to educate individuals *for* society: it could be equally be argued that the teachers' job is to encourage pupils to change society or at least be critical of certain aspects of it. One very important tradition in the teaching of English, for example, suggests that the task of education is not to reflect the standards of society (as portrayed in the mass media), but to offer children something better — that is, literature rather than sub-standard fiction or reporting. The second fallacy is that the society-centred justification begs the whole question about the nature of society. Society is a collection of the individual members, so it is necessary to ask 'who decides that society needs more technicians . . .?' The idea of society needing something different from the needs of individual members is very curious; the idea of teachers or the education system 'producing' desirable adults, in the same way as a factory produces motor cars, is a very dangerous analogy.

The point that I am trying to make is that whilst there may be some truth in each of these three views of education and curriculum – the child-centred, the knowledge-centred and the society-centred – none of them is a complete view or model in its own right. The child-centred view can best be seen as a desirable reaction against harsh practices of earlier centuries, together with a recognition of stages of child-development and the need to recognise childhood as of value in its own right as well as a preparation for adult life. Knowledge as represented by subjects also has an important part to play, but the way in which knowledge is structured and organised, together with some kind of system of putting knowledge into priorities, also needs to be examined and justified. Finally, we cannot ignore the fact that we live in an industrial, technological society, but education should not be dominated by the needs of the economy: there is more to education than preparing individuals for their working life. Education should also be concerned with leisure and creative abilities as well as with being a member of society as a whole.

What is therefore needed is a much more comprehensive view of the curriculum, a view that will take into account the merits of the three approaches outlined above, and weld them together in an integrated approach to curriculum planning. It may also be important to point out at this stage that there is no necessary conflict between the needs of the individual and the supposed needs of society, as many progressive educationists seem to have assumed. The individual can only become truly human and social by becoming a member of a community and a social group. A child growing up in isolation from the rest of humanity can only be seen as a child who becomes sub-human.The essence of full humanity is sharing in the language, culture and experiences of other human beings. A curriculum should therefore aim at introducing the individual child to the world of other human beings through appropriate kinds of knowledge and experience. That is essentially the approach adopted by those curriculum theorists whose system is based on 'cultural analysis'.[7]

Cultural Analysis

My own approach is based on the definition of curriculum as a selection from the culture of society. Culture in this context is used in the anthropological or sociological sense of everything that is man-made in our society – fish and chips and bingo as well as science and mathematics; values and beliefs as well as religion, art and literature; pop culture as well as high culture, and so on. No school can possibly teach everything, or pass the whole of our culture on to the next generation, so decisions have to be made about priorities. We have to make a selection from everything in our culture and plan a curriculum to pass on to the next generation the most important aspects of our cultural heritage. It should perhaps be stressed that this is not a static view of culture – the essence of culture in a society like ours is that it is constantly changing. The school also has a responsibility to take account of that change, but not necessarily to reflect all kinds of change. Value judgments have to be made about the kinds of change which are necessary and important, and those kinds of change which should be resisted. This is related to the remark I made about the tradition in English teaching of making decisions about the quality of the materials made available to pupils. The following model necessarily over-simplifies these processes, but may provide a useful guide to curriculum planning under certain conditions.

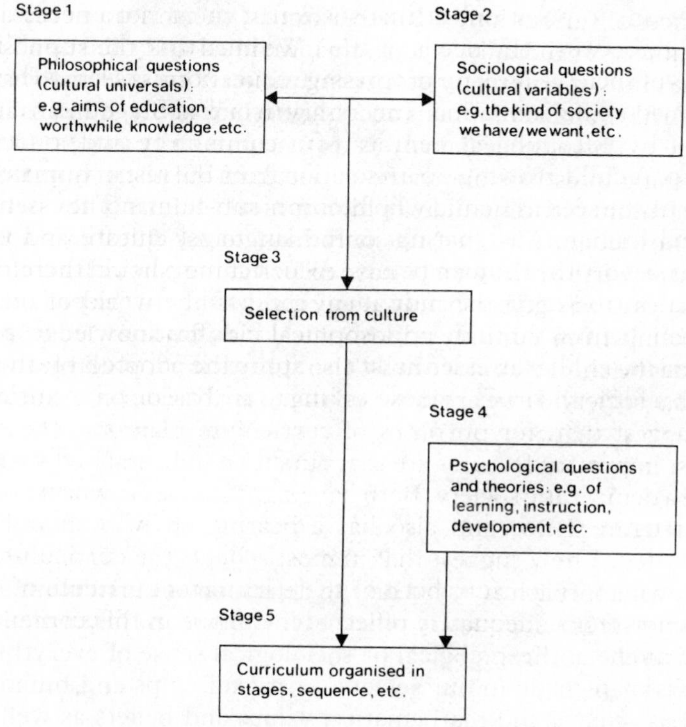

Stages 1 and 2

There are some questions which might be described as mainly but not exclusively philosophical, which will apply to education and curricula in any society. At one level we have to ask questions about the meaning and purpose of education. Philosophers may tell us that education must make people 'better' in some way (but what counts as better may be influenced by the particular stage in its history). At another level we say that education is concerned with the transmission of worthwhile knowledge and experiences; but definitions of worthwhile may not be purely educational – they may be contaminated by social class values or prejudices (Stage 2). Thus if a boy is good at cricket, make him a prefect – if he is good at snooker, expel him! At a third level we have to ask questions about the structure of knowledge; there are probably good arguments for saying that mathematics and history really are identifiably different kinds of knowledge, but the difference between, say, geography and geology is to some extent arbitrary and a result of social traditions and influences of various kinds. In other words, we cannot assume that all subjects are equally 'watertight'. We need to try and establish some kinds of criteria for discussing various kinds of knowledge.

We have already found it necessary to look at Stage 2 as well as Stage 1. Philosophical analysis may help us to be more rational in asking questions about the curriculum but there is more to curriculum planning than a philosophical analysis of the nature of knowledge. Also, we not only have to ask questions about what is worthwhile, we also have to look at the particular characteristics of any given society at any given time. In the process of selecting from culture, philosophical clarification can help to guide the choices, but we must also study the particular features of that society. If we are now seeking to analyse our own society, I suggest that, for purposes of curriculum planning, the two most important features are that ours is an industralised society and a democratic society. Both have significance for what should be taught; the second also has a bearing on who should be educated. I now suggest that in most schools the curriculum is unsatisfactory because both of these important features of our society are not adequately reflected in the process of curriculum planning.

Stage 3

The interplay between Stages 1 and 2 will enable us to make an ideal selection from the culture (Stage 3). I would want to suggest that everyone's curriculum should include mathematics and the sciences, not simply because they exist as forms of knowledge, but because they are particularly important kinds of knowledge in the society in which we live. Without a basic understanding of this kind of knowledge, I would maintain that an individual cannot understand and, therefore, cannot play a full part in the life of our society. For similar reasons, no curriculum could be regarded as complete without the humanities and social sciences. Everyone should understand something about the history of his own society (as well as other people's); he should also understand the political, economic and social structure of his own country in relation to others. I would also regard a curriculum as basically deficient if it did not include a strong aesthetic element: man is essentially a creative animal and education should seek to develop expressive talents over a much wider range of subjects than most schools offer at the moment.

You will have noticed that some of the elements in the curriculum which I have mentioned are 'subjects'; others are much broader aspects of human experience. I want to assert that education is not primarily concerned with passing on 'subjects' or subject matter, but should be concerned with much broader aims or objectives. Subjects are normally the means by which we attain these objectives rather than having the status of objectives themselves.

Stage 4

The next stage is to begin thinking about how to achieve these aims in practice. Stage 4 takes us in that direction. Once we have decided on the ideal selection from the culture, it is necessary to give a good deal of attention to the practical organisation of transmitting this culture. We need to know how children think, how they learn, how they can be motivated. A good deal is known, for example, from the work of Piaget[8] and other psychologists, about the stages of development that children pass through. We know that children need to have concrete understanding before they pass on to abstract problems.

Stage 5

Finally, we reach Stage 5 and the curriculum organised in terms of sequence, stages of development and perhaps subjects. Subjects come at the end of the story not at the beginning.

A Common Culture

This view of the curriculum sees the child at the centre surrounded by 'culture' and the teacher having the job of acting as mediator. It is the teacher's task to provide the developing child with those kinds of experiences and those kinds of knowledge which will help him to develop as a full member of the society to which he belongs. Decisions have to be made about what kinds of knowledge and what kinds of experience are both worthwhile and relevant to the developing individual at particular stages. In a democratic society, we also make the assertion that all children should have this kind of opportunity. Seen in this way, education becomes a process of making available to all young people those kinds of experiences which are regarded as educationally worthwhile. Education thus becomes a matter of 'right of access to knowledge' rather than packages of information which are imposed upon the young by their teachers. If the curriculum is seen as a set of rights,[9] then the task of the teacher is revolutionised but not made any easier. The teacher still has to make demands on pupils that they would not make on themselves if the teacher were not there. Unfortunately, children do not always 'naturally' seek what is good for them – they have to be guided. Although the curriculum may be a set of rights, children still have to be not only told what their rights are, but also urged to take advantage of what is available. This is not always easy. Teachers are still very necessary. In the child-centred model teachers are all but redundant; in the cultural analysis model the teacher's role is changed, but is even more important.

The teacher's responsibility is to make available to every child aspects of the common culture of our society. This is based on the view that, although every child is an individual, and every family is different, and communities have interesting unique features, there still is something which we call a common culture. Without a common culture, a society ceases to exist. Despite regional, religious, ethnic and other differences, there must be certain basic kinds of values which are respected and kinds of knowledge which are important for all members of the society. The common curriculum[10] is a selection from that common culture. It is based on what everyone needs to know or what everyone ought to have access to. It is not a uniform curriculum since different individuals will reach different stages of understanding or appreciation. For example, we may agree that everyone ought to have a basic understanding of science in order to understand our society, but it would be extremely foolish to try to make everyone have exactly the same kind of understanding. Some will reach no more than minimum competence; others will become Nobel Prize winners in physics.

One difficulty which is often raised in connection with the idea of a common curriculum is that we live in a pluralistic society. The assumption then being made is that if we do not agree on all values and all beliefs, a common culture does not exist and a common curriculum is theoretically impossible. This is a misunderstanding of the common culture and common curriculum idea. The common culture view is based on the fact that, *despite* differences of values, beliefs and ways of life, there must be certain values and so on which people do share, otherwise society would cease to exist. The process of cultural analysis is precisely concerned with identifying those aspects of culture which are common and to set them aside from those which are diverse. This can be very difficult, but it is an essential process of curriculum planning.

It has been objected, for example, that working-class[11] communities do not share the values of middle-class educators, and that this is the reason for so much educational failure. There may be an element of truth in this, but I would want to reject the basic assumption that there is nothing in common between the so-called middle-class culture and working-class culture. To make such an assertion is to mistake the part for the whole. At one level it can be established that we share such major aspects of culture as language (despite regional and class variations); at another level, it is important to recognise the universality of certain aspects of culture such as mathematics and science – in what sense could we possibly say that physics is middle class or working class? The confusion arises from the undoubted fact that there are differences in taste which are partly (but not wholly) class related. Certain kinds of literature, certain kinds of music can be shown to be appreciated by some sections of society more than others, but two points have to be made immediately. The first is that the greatest differences are concerned with relatively trivial aspects of culture rather than basic components (pigeon-breeding being mainly working class; horse-breeding upper class); second, that most of the assertions about class-related taste are based on statistics which show correlations between class and activities (say, opera-going) which concern tiny minorities. In other words, it is true that more middle-class adults go to Covent Garden than working-class adults, but only a tiny minority of middle-class people are interested in opera; similarly, it is certainly not true that no working-class people are interested in opera.

What we have to concentrate on are those major aspects of culture which we can demonstrate as being:

(a) worthwhile;
(b) extremely important in our society; and
(c) necessary for the whole community.

We would then reject the idea of a special working-class curriculum for pupils in working-class areas, although we would not rule out the possibility of certain fringe activities being available within the school curriculum. This is also to make a distinction between a national curriculum plan and the curriculum as organised in individual schools. If we believe in a common curriculum, then there are clearly some aspects of knowledge which ought to be available in all schools; on the other hand, there are certain kinds of experience which will be much more relevant in some areas and for some children than for others. To assert the idea of a national common curriculum is not to advocate a uniform curriculum without any local or teacher-based variation.

Curriculum in a Multi-cultural Society

A final question relates to the problem of a common curriculum in a multi-cultural society. In some respects, the arguments here are identical to those applied to the problem of social class differences above. However, it is important to look at the question of a multi-cultural society since some of the aspects of this argument are distint from the question of social class and regional differences.

The problem of a multi-cultural society (if it is a problem rather than a potential enrichment) is that the society contains groups of individuals, perhaps even small communities, which do not share some of the beliefs, attitudes or knowledge priorities of the host community. In England, for example, we have large numbers of immigrants or children of immigrants whose first language is not English. They may also have religious values which do not coincide with the beliefs of the majority of the population. Two kinds of problem emerge from this situation. The first is, what kinds of common curriculum can be made available which would not offend these minority groups? The second is that there ought to be an element of the common curriculum which will help the majority as well as the minorities to understand each other better, and therefore produce a more cohesive society.

To some extent the arguments I have already applied to the social class differences also apply to a multi-cultural society. It can be said that whatever background children come from they will need, growing up in our society, to develop an understanding of mathematics, of science, of technology, of politics and economics, in order to live fully and participate in that society. If children from cultural minorities are not given access to those kinds of knowledge, then they are being deprived of the opportunity to become full members of society. The same argument applies to language: if they are to live and participate in mainstream British society, they must acquire a high degree of competence in the English language. The focus of attention then switches away from the major elements of the common curriculum to the question of 'what else should go into the curriculum?'

Schools must also face the question of what efforts they will make to encourage children to respect, and to develop within, their own culture: to acquire competence in their native language as well as English, and to develop a taste for their own literature and music as well as the content of the common curriculum. These are extremely important questions to which general answers cannot be given, but teachers should certainly become more aware of them. But they should pay attention to these problems in the context of a common curriculum not as a substitute for it. There is increasing evidence to show that teachers can do a good deal of damage by focusing on the minority culture at the expense of, instead of in addition to, the common curriculum or common culture. For example, it has been shown that some teachers, perhaps with the best of intentions, have tried to use their own limited knowledge of, say, Caribbean dialects to encourage West Indian children to respect and use that form of English.[12] This may result in the parents of those children objecting to the fact that their children do not learn how to read and write in standard English which they see, rightly, as the major task of the school.

As for the content of the common curriculum which ought to encourage harmony between the various groups, a distinction needs to be made between what might be recommended nationally and what is better left for local arrangements or even arrangements within individual schools. It is certainly true that a general recommendation should be made to encourage all schools to include materials which would foster respect for cultures other than our own. This can be achieved through 'subjects' such as history (not focusing exclusively on British or Imperial history; not talking about discovering America without adequately explaining that there were inhabitants there with a culture of their own before the Europeans arrived, and so on). In addition, many social studies programmes at primary and secondary level now include work of an elementary anthropological nature with the specific intention of inculcating respect for other cultures. Handled with care this kind of curriculum development can be very beneficial, but a good deal of attention needs to be paid to the particular materials provided and the attitudes used by teachers. It is too easy to fall into the trap of being patronising or of concentrating on the least important aspect of other cultures such as housing or dress. Certain principles and guidelines could be agreed nationally, but most of the work will be subject to local variations and arrangements made within individual schools.

It is sometimes suggested that there are three different kinds of educational response to the problem of minority ethnic groups. These may be described as assimilation, integration, and cultural pluralism.

Twenty years or so ago, the idea of assimilation was seen as the answer to the problem of immigration. It was felt that a period of disorientation and culture shock (including lack of knowledge of English) should be treated on a specific basis and that then the problems of immigrants would simply disappear. In other words, assimilation depended simply on competence in English as a second language, and possibly as a first language for the next generation. Minority groups would be assimilated as soon as they could speak our language: problems of culture and colour could be ignored.

It soon became apparent, however, that minority groups were not simply absorbed into the mainstream culture. At this stage, cultural differences were recognised, but the problem was seen simply as making native-born English children aware of these differences and encouraging them to tolerate variations from their own culture in life style and religion and in other ways. Teachers were a key element in this kind of integration programme, and courses were often arranged for them. In London, for example, small groups of teachers were encouraged to go for short periods of familiarisation to the West Indies or India. The emphasis at this stage was to give teachers, and ultimately native-born pupils, sufficient knowledge of, and sympathy for, the culture of the ethnic minorities to encourage respect and harmony. This kind of programme had some good results and enabled teachers to prepare materials which would familiarise pupils with the positive aspects of other cultures such as Islam, the arts of the Indian sub-continent, and West Indian music and dancing. But this approach was often superficial and at worst paternalistic, and patronising.

The final approach, cultural pluralism, is based on the idea that ethic minorities should not be expected either to be assimilated or to be integrated, thus losing their cultural differences, but should be encouraged to preserve and foster their cultures. In terms of curriculum planning, this means that the common curriculum should be devised in such a way as to provide all groups, native-born and the children of ethnic minorities, with the kind of knowledge necessary for our society, but it should also be concerned with a much broader content, teaching about different religions, cultures, as well as problems of race relations for all pupils. In addition, it is necessary to plan for the specific educational needs of the minority groups. These will not only be the teaching of English, but also be concerned with the specific difficulties encountered in mathematics and in science. The assumption underlying this approach is that the children of ethnic minorities are not simply a nuisance in our schools, but present an enrichment of our own culture. It is certainly true, however, that an adequate curriculum will not emerge spontaneously even from a good deal of practical experience; curriculum planning is vital if this approach is to be successful.[13]

Summary

The definition of the curriculum as 'a selection from the culture of a society' is uncontroversial. What else could it be? The controversy arises when we start deciding on the process of selection. At this stage values are inevitable. It is impossible to have a 'value-free' curriculum, but values should be made explicit and justified in rational terms. When judged in this way the traditional curriculum is seen to be unsatisfactory in a number of ways. Later chapters will discuss other aspects of curriculum planning.

NOTES

1 **There have also been criticisms** about the control of the curriculum. In 1976, Ann Corbett in the Fabian Society's evidence to the Taylor Committee suggested that the curriculum was too important to be left to teachers and that reformed governing bodies ought to exercise more local control over the curriculum. Raison (1976) stated that it was unfortunate that the 1944 Education Act had failed to lay down any curricular guidelines. *See* Lawton (1980).

2 **'Comprehensive'** in this context is used with two overlapping meanings: it will be a curriculum designed to cater for a wide range of abilities; it will also be a curriculum covering a wide range of content.

3 **Some of these 'progressive' points of view** in education will be examined in greater detail in Chapter 8.

4 **Plowden Report:** Report of the Central Advisory Council for Education (England) *Children and their Primary Schools* (Chairman, Lady Bridget Plowden). In 1963, the CACE was given the following terms of reference: to consider primary education in all its aspects, and the transition to secondary education.

The Report recommended that the structure of primary education should be changed to first schools (age 5 to 8) followed by middle schools (age 8 to 12). This has not been generally accepted though it was taken up by a number of LEAs. The Report recommended the 'progressive' viewpoint on primary education and curriculum. It criticised those schools where there was a rigid division of the curriculum into subjects. Approval was given to the topic approach rather than a curriculum based on subjects or subject areas. The Report was, almost immediately, criticised by a number of educationists for its naive acceptance of the progressive viewpoint. *See* Peters (1968).

5 **For example, Neville Bennett** (1976) examined the relationship between teaching styles and primary children's performance in the basic subjects. One of the interesting by-products of this research was that it was relatively uncommon to find primary schools practising extreme versions of the progressive ideology. This was borne out by the HMI survey *Primary Education in England* (1978).

6 **The HMI Report** *Aspects of Secondary Education in England*

(1979) is usually referred to as the Secondary School Survey. The Survey concentrated on the final two years of compulsory schooling (14 to 16). The Survey was planned as a series of inspections of a 10% sample of maintained secondary schools. Four aspects of education were scrutinised: language skills, mathematical understanding and competence, scientific skills and understanding, and the personal and social development of the pupils. The system of planning a curriculum for the fourteen to sixteen age group by means of a system of options was very much criticised by HMI.

7 **The tradition of cultural analysis** goes back in England at least as far as Matthew Arnold (1822-88) whose book *Culture and Anarchy* has been a continuing (if controversial) influence. Raymond Williams continued and developed this tradition, in a very different way, in *Culture and Society* (1958) and *The Long Revolution* (1961). In the USA, perhaps the most interesting book is *Democracy and Excellence in American Secondary Education* (Broudy, Smith, and Burnett, 1964). What all these approaches have in common is an intention to derive a common curriculum from a common culture. The process of derivation (or selection) is, however, often implicit rather than explicit. My own view is that the process of selection from the culture has to be made explicit by some kind of system of cultural analysis.

8 **Jean Piaget** (1896-1980) is one of the most influential figures in educational psychology, although he regarded himself primarily as a genetic epistemologist — that is, a biologist interested in the problem of how knowledge emerges and develops in human consciousness. Piaget's work in developmental psychology will be further discussed in Chapter 3.

9 **Rights.** The question of the curriculum seen as a set of rights will be discussed in Chapter 6. Briefly stated, the argument is that if education is compulsory then those whose liberty is thereby removed have a right to some benefit in return. This right or benefit must include a worthwhile curriculum which is, to some extent, specified.

10 **Common Curriculum.** I have made a distinction between a common curriculum and a uniform curriculum. It may also be necessary to emphasise a distinction between the common curriculum and a core curriculum. The core curriculum is a low level concept which simply states the desirability of a small number of subjects being included in the curriculum for all children. The 1979 Secondary School Survey showed that when most headteachers claimed that they had a core curriculum this only meant that mathematics and English were compulsory for all children. The danger with a core curriculum is that it can become the whole curriculum.

11 **In** *Class, Culture and the Curriculum* (Lawton 1975) I examined in some detail the argument about whether there should be a working class curriculum for working class children. I had no doubt about rejecting the view put forward by Bantock (1975) in his paper

'Towards a Theory of Popular Education' that there should be a non-academic curriculum for the majority of children.

12 **Some of the evidence** referred to is contained in Maureen Stone's Ph. D. thesis (1978), *Black Culture, Self Concept and Schooling* (University of Surrey). Maureen Stone's research has now been published under the title *Education of the Black Child in Britain* by Fontana (1981).

13 *See* Robert Jeffcoate (1977).

3 Teaching and Learning in School

In Chapter 2, I outlined some of the approaches to planning a curriculum which have been recommended in recent years. However, a well-planned curriculum is no guarantee that learning takes place. For that to happen it is also necessary to have a teacher who is competent and a pupil who is reasonably well motivated. An incompetent teacher can destroy any teaching programme, however well prepared; an unwilling pupil can resist the most assiduous attempts to teach him. How can teaching and learning be improved, given these constraints?

The effective teacher needs to know a good deal not only about what he is teaching, but also how children learn. In planning the curriculum as a whole we have to ask questions about the structure of knowledge; at another level, in planning the work of a teacher or group of teachers, we have to ask questions about the structure of a discipline or a subject: its key concepts, validation procedures and logical structure.

The Structure of Subject Matter

A fundamental criticism of traditional methods of teaching and learning is that too much emphasis is placed on memorising facts with too little attention paid to understanding. I learnt chemistry at school in just that way: learning by rote symbols and formulae; writing down accounts of experiments I had never performed myself, and sometimes never seen. Having a good memory, I could do what was required and passed an examination at the end; but of the nature of chemistry as a branch of science I understood almost nothing.

It would be easy to go to the other extreme and say that children should never be required to rote learn anything, and must discover everything for themselves. This would be equally foolish, although something like it is often recommended in some teacher training programmes. What teachers have to be able to do is to select from the vast mass of information available in any subject those key features which give understanding as well as provide the basis for future learning. Whatever a teacher is trying to impart, he must ask first, 'why is this important?; second, 'what are the key ideas, concepts, principles involved?'; and third, 'what is the best sequence?' The assumption underlying those three questions is that the subject matter or content is often less important for its own sake than as a kind of building block to provide a base for future learning.

It is perhaps important to make a somewhat artificial distinction between the overlapping categories of knowledge and experience at this stage. There are many educational experiences which are worth while in their own right — for example, reading a poem, listening to music, solving a mathematical problem. But even while recognising the importance of experience in its own right, the good teacher will try to select experiences (poems, music, problems, and so on) which will tend to lead on to other worthwhile experiences, rather than simply be enjoyed for their own sake. School time is so limited, and therefore so valuable, that a good teacher will plan carefully to get the most out of every minute of the teaching day, and like a good chess player, be thinking three or four moves ahead.

Jerome Bruner, the American psychologist and educationist, has contributed a good deal on this topic. In addition to two books which are of very particular relevance, *The Process*[1] *of Education* (Bruner 1960) and *Toward a Theory of Instruction* (Bruner 1966) Bruner initiated a very important social studies curriculum project for schools, *Man, a Course of Study,* which put into practice some of his ideas about structure, sequence and key concepts. The content of the course, as the title suggests, is 'man'. Bruner specifies this in the following way:

> . . . his nature as a species, the forces that shape and continue to shape his humanity.

Three questions recur throughout the course:

1 What is human about human beings?
2 How did they get that way?
3 How can they be made more so?

The structure of the course, following these three questions, is arranged around the exploration of five topics, each associated with the evolution of man as a species. These are referred to by Bruner as five 'humanising forces':

(a) tool-making;
(b) language;
(c) social organisation;
(d) the management of man's prolonged childhood;
(e) man's urge to explain his world.

Bruner proceeds to show that each one of these five areas contains key concepts that relate with other concepts, such as the notion of 'tool', which is not immediately understood by young children, or perhaps even by some adults.

So, for Bruner, teaching a pupil social studies (or any other subject area) is not simply providing him with information and facts to store, but involves teaching a child to think in a way that a social scientist would think. But how can that be made possible?

> Mastery of the fundamental ideas of a field involves not only the grasping of general principles, but also the development of an attitude toward learning and enquiry, toward guessing and hunches, toward the possibility of solving problems on one's own.

Clearly it is very important not to go to extremes in this, thereby misinterpreting Bruner's very important message. No child, left to his own process of 'discovery',[2] can produce a structure in science or social studies which will have taken hundreds or thousands of years of expert work to evolve; the teacher's job is to provide short cuts to significant learning; guided discovery, not blind groping in the dark, is the correct teaching formula. The art of teaching is to enable children to make discoveries they would not encounter on their own.

Bruner's Theory of Instruction

According to Bruner, a theory of instruction has four major features which can be considered under the following headings: predispositions to learning; the structure and form of knowledge; sequence; reinforcement.

Predispositions to learning

A theory of instruction should specify those early experiences which would be most likely to produce a predisposition to learning: for example, the kinds of relationships with people and things in the pre-school environment which will tend to make the child willing and able to learn in school. Such influences will include cultural influences, and motivational and personal factors. This places a very great burden on the teacher: he must understand something about the cultural background of his pupils, what makes them want to learn or not want to learn, and be informed about individual personal characteristics. Some of these the teacher may be able to influence, others he may simply become more aware of and make allowance for.

Learning and problem solving depend on exploration of alternatives. If curiosity is seen as the response of children to ambiguity and uncertainty, then there are three important aspects involved for teachers to make the best use of curiosity in any learning situation:

1 *Activation* (the teacher may need to arouse curiosity);
2 *Maintenance* (the teacher must know how to keep interest alive and keep an exploration going when left to himself the child might lose interest);
3 *Direction* (preventing enquiry from becoming random); direction will depend on the teacher helping the pupil to have clear-cut goals and also providing feedback or knowledge of the pupil's success so far.

Structure and form of knowledge

A theory of instruction involves specifying the ways in which knowledge should be structured for the learner. Bruner is not referring here to the philosophical problem of the structure and organisation of knowledge: he is talking about the relationship between the knowledge which the teacher thinks should be acquired by the pupil and the nature of the learner as a particular individual. A careful matching process is required. There will be some general rules applicable to all children, but the teacher must also be aware of the individual differences noted above. Bruner believes that any idea or problem can be presented in a form simple enough for any particular learner to understand. The teacher's skill in presentation, depending on his knowledge of the pupil, is crucial.

The structure of any domain of knowledge may be characterised in three ways:

the mode of representation;
its economy;
its power.

Each of these will affect the ability of a pupil to master knowledge. All three vary according to the age and learning style of a pupil as well as according to the subject matter:

(a) The mode of representation will depend on the child's stage of development and will be more or less concrete or abstract.

(b) Economy in representing knowledge refers to the amount of information which a pupil must have and work with in order to understand. For example, it is more economical to express certain mathematical relations as a formula than by pages of worked examples. But children have to begin with examples (that is, at a stage of less economy) and work their way gradually to a stage of greater economy — abstract symbols, and so on.

(c) The power of any way of structuring knowledge for learning can be seen as its capacity for enabling the learner to make connections between matters otherwise seen quite separately (that is, knowledge should be seen in terms of its power to increase the potentiality for more knowledge).

Sequence

A theory of instruction should specify the most effective sequence for learning specific kinds of knowledge. Sequence is of two kinds. The first relates to logical sequence within the subject matter; the second refers to the kind of sequence which the teacher should be aware of in the pupil's mind — that is, proceeding from the concrete to the abstract or symbolic.

It will also be necessary for teachers to know when a sequential structure is important and when it can be ignored. Most of Bruner's examples are taken from mathematics and science where structure and sequence are very powerful, but it may be that in other kinds of learning, sequence is much less important. A good deal of research remains to be done in this area.

The form and pacing of reinforcement

A theory of instruction will specify the nature and pacing of rewards and punishments. As learning progresses, it will be better to shift away from extrinsic rewards (for example, teachers' praise) to intrinsic rewards (solving a problem for its own sake). Also, teachers should know when to replace immediate rewards by deferred rewards. The timing of these two shifts are poorly understood by teachers. Many studies have shown that teachers either tend to give very little reward (praise) or to reward indiscriminately; the good teacher paces his rewards carefully and is not afraid to criticise where necessary, and where advisable.

Bruner's theory of instruction is concerned with three factors:

(a) the nature of the knowledge to be learned;[3]
(b) the nature of the learning process in general terms;
(c) the need to be aware of individual children's specific needs.

The reason why teaching is so difficult is that the inter-action of these three factors is so complex, in many cases, that every learning situation must be regarded as unique. But at the same time teachers should be able to make generalisations and be able to apply them. Unfortunately, most discussions about streaming and non-streaming, group learning, individual learning, class learning, and so on are carried on without sufficient attention being paid to the three factors.

How Children Develop

A good deal of Bruner's recommendations rely on the teacher having a competent understanding of 'what makes children tick', at various ages or stages of development. One of his major contributions has been his stress on the necessary inter-relatedness of the structure of knowledge and the structure of learning behaviour. Teaching then becomes partly a matter of matching these two sets of factors. Unfortunately, in England, and in most other countries, we have tended to think that it is necessary for primary school teachers to 'understand child development', but not to know much about the structure of knowledge, whereas secondary school teachers are expected to be experts in their own subject field, but not to know very much about children's cognitive development. This failure explains a good deal of unsatisfactory teaching in primary and secondary schools alike.

Cognitive development

Piaget's[4] is the name which dominates this field. Unfortunately his work has been misunderstood, over-simplified, misinterpreted and badly applied in schools (if it is not completely ignored). In order to do justice to Piaget it is important to stress that he did not see himself primarily as an educational psychologist, but as an epistemologist — he was interested in how knowledge acquired is related to mental structures, not how best to teach children arithmetic. Nevertheless, his work is of great relevance to teachers, and a basic knowledge of Piaget's theories and experiments should be regarded as a pre-requisite for any qualified teacher.

Apart from the stages of development, which have been a major source of misinterpretation of Piaget, a number of principles for teaching and learning can be derived from the work of Piaget and his followers. First, children's learning should be an active process — that is, a teacher can guide, help, and discuss difficulties with a pupil, but eventually the pupil must think for himself. This does not, of course, mean that a classroom where children are running about is a better learning environment than one in which they are sitting still. Quite the opposite: activity does not necessarily mean physical activity, still less violent activity, but simply 'thinking it out', maybe with the help of physical objects, maybe not. The teacher's task is to present the child with situations which require 'experimentation' and the drawing of conclusions. It would probably be better to refer to this as a problem-solving approach to learning rather than as 'discovery'. What we think of as intelligent behaviour does not simply mature as children grow older. Piaget conceived of this as a cumulative process of building up more and more complex and flexible 'schemata',[5] which depend on active exploration by the child in response to arousal and reinforcement by the child's environment. Piaget's studies have mapped out the kinds of mental processes characteristic of children at various stages: the sensori-motor responses soon after birth; the illogical notions and limited reasoning of the pre-school child; the more realistic thinking (concrete operations) of older children; and, finally, the rational and scientific problem-solving (formal operations) of intelligent adolescents and adults.

One of the important features of Piaget's work is that it has shown (confirming some of the notions of Rousseau and others) that the baby does not perceive a world of objects which remain the same regardless of the angle of perception or the distance (and also regardless of his own desires). Piaget demonstrated that this kind of understanding is not innate but has to be acquired during the first few years of life by seeing, touching, and exploring objects. What many adults take for granted, such as concepts of space, time and number, are still only partly formed among children of seven or eight. Such concepts have to be acquired slowly, constantly corrected and extended through interaction with adults and other children, but above all, through practical experience.

A second major idea derived from Piaget is that effective learning is often social rather than individual. Other children can often provide more appropriate stimulation than adults. Teachers are generally poor at constructing tasks for social learning, and the dominant learning situation still tends to be teacher talking and children learning (or pretending to listen). This tendency has not been helped by such recent practices in schools as 'individualised learning' and 'computer-assisted learning', where pupils usually have no opportunity even for informal (or illegal) consultations with their peers.

A third principle is derived from the stages of development referred to above: that is, the much abused concept of 'readiness'. Children should not be forced to work at a stage which they have not yet reached. This view has, however, sometimes been misinterpreted by teachers in a way which enables them to abdicate from their responsibilities. They may refuse to teach a child until he is 'ready to learn'. This is a complete misunderstanding of Piaget — what the teacher ought to be doing is preparing the child to learn by assisting him at the earlier stage. In particular, the phrase 'reading readiness' has been much used and abused. Teachers have been known to stand by and just wait for children to ask to learn to read. The true interpetation of Piaget would be for the teacher to concentrate on pre-reading skills and encourage the development of readiness rather than simply wait for it to happen.

Bruner[6] also operates with a cognitive development model. His terminology is different from Piaget and is perhaps more acceptable to teachers. Bruner sees development in terms of evolution: he sees man's technological progress as having produced three systems which act as amplifiers of human capacities. These are amplifiers of human *motor* capacities (for example, a knife or weapon or tool); amplifiers of human *sensory* capacities (from smoke signals to drums, radio and television); finally, amplifiers of human *thought* processes (from language to myth to scientific theory).

Similarly, Bruner describes child development in terms of 'levels of knowing'. The three stages or levels are 'enactive, iconic and symbolic'. Children develop enactive powers before iconic, and iconic before the symbolic. Mature adults will use all three, but not necessarily be at the same level of development in all spheres of life.

The three modes of representation may be illustrated as follows:

> A very young child can *act* on the basis of the principles of a balance beam as he plays on a seesaw. He understands that to get his side of the seesaw to go further down, he has to move out further from the centre. He is at the enactive level or using the enactive mode of representation. An older child can *represent* the balance beam by a model on which rings can be hung and balanced, or even by a drawing of a balance. The image of the balance beam can be refined to the stage of a diagram in a physics textbook. This is the iconic mode.
>
> Finally, a balance beam can be *described* by means of language, without diagrams, or can be described mathematically by reference to Newton's Law of Moments of Inertia in physics. This is the symbolic mode of representation available only to intelligent adolescents or adults who have learned the necessary skills.

Peel's View of Cognitive Growth

Professor Edwin Peel's work on adolescent thinking is extremely important for secondary school teachers, but badly neglected by them and also by the writers of textbooks and examination questions. Peel (1968) set out his view of cognitive growth, derived from Piaget, but applied directly to the kind of work which children are expected to do in school. His studies seem to show that probably Piaget's ages for reaching formal operations or the ability to tackle abstract problems were optimistic. Peel studied carefully the way that secondary school pupils' ability changes from early to middle and late adolescence. In terms of the kinds of tasks which are set in secondary schools, Peel says that concrete thinking is associated with description whereas formal thought is necessary for explanation.

When a pupil is able to explain as well as merely describe, this represents a significant change in his ability. This is not simply an ability to explain a specific example, but also to generalise and to suggest a hypothesis and test it. Peel stresses, however, that hypotheses do not arise spontaneously; it is necessary for teachers to provide plenty of practical and concrete experience in order to bring pupils up to the stage of explanation.

Another point made by Peel is that many secondary schools differ sharply in terms of method and curriculum planning from what pupils have become accustomed to in primary schools. He stresses the need for transition periods, and suggests that in the first two years of the secondary school there is still considerable need for the concrete in mathematics and science. Science teachers should also not expect explanation but should be content with description of results in these early secondary years.

In a later book, Peel (1971) investigates the nature of adolescent judgment. Peel suggests that understanding is not enough in secondary education, but that we must proceed to the all-important stage of being able to make effective judgments. In his analysis of adolescent judgment, Peel suggests that pupils' responses tend to fall into three basic categories:

(a) restricted;
(b) circumstantial;
(c) imaginative-comprehensive.

These three categories are associated with chronological and mental age.

Level 1 responses (restricted) were made by only a few of the twelve-year-old pupils tested; age thirteen to fourteen was associated with the second level (circumstantial) where logical but restricted judgments were given to the information. Level 3 was reached by pupils of about fifteen years of age or older. These findings have an important implication, not only for individual teachers but also for curriculum planners. Many of the very desirable kinds of judgments which secondary school pupils ought to be able to make before they leave school are only just within the grasp of many of those in their final year at school. For example, political and moral judgments of an advanced kind would only be possible for many pupils in their final year at school, and for some pupils even after that. This has clear implications for the school leaving age or policies for day release studies at Further Education colleges for those who leave at the earliest possible date.

Lawrence Kohlberg and Moral Development

The work of Kohlberg in the USA applies the ideas of Piaget and others to the specific field of moral development. Kohlberg and his associates at Harvard University studied a group of seventy-five boys for twelve years, mapping out the stages of their moral thinking during that time. The boys were aged between ten and sixteen at the beginning of the study, reaching 22 to 28 by the end of the programme. Kohlberg has also explored moral development in other cultures. Kohlberg's technique was to present the boys with moral problems for discussion; he taped the answers and analysed them. As a result of this study, Kohlberg set out a scheme describing the general structure of moral development.

According to Kohlberg there are three main levels of moral thinking, and within each stage, two levels:

1 Pre-moral

Stage A: the child is orientated to punishment and obedience.

Stage B: 'naive instrumental hedonism'.

Rewards are still important but the child is beginning to be conditioned and to generalise in this category.

2 Level of conventional rule conformity

Stage C: 'good boy orientation'. Good behaviour is what is approved by others. Conformity to sterotyped images of what is natural or the view of the majority. A significant change is that *intention* becomes an important consideration. A child seeks approval by doing what he imagines others would like him to do.

Stage D: orientation towards authority, fixed rules and the maintenance of social order. Correct behaviour or moral behaviour now consists of doing one's duty, showing respect for authority.

3 Level of morality of self-accepted moral principles (post conventional level)

Stage E: the morality of contract. Moral action tends to be defined in terms of general rights and standards accepted by the whole society. This is a 'legalistic point of view, but laws are now seen as changeable rather than static as in Stage D.

Stage F : the morality of the individual principles of conscience. At this stage, principles are now abstract and in accordance with ethical standards.

It is difficult to attach ages to these stages of development since individuals appear to vary according to social class and intelligence. But teachers would do well to be aware of the general outline of Kohlberg's findings. It is also apparently the case that even adults may be at an advanced stage of development for one aspect of their lives, but 'regress' to a lower stage when faced with different kinds of problem.

Individual Differences

Having established some general principles about the kind of knowledge which teachers ought to possess about children's development, we should now look at some of the important aspects in which children of roughly the same age may differ. This has, of course, already been referred to in connection with Bruner and others.

Individual ability or intelligence

The 1944 Education Act specified that children should be educated according to age, ability and aptitude. This seemingly obvious phrase has caused a good deal of trouble ever since. Age appears to be a matter of little dispute, but what about ability and aptitude? It is obvious that people differ in their abilities as well as in their achievements, but many who are extremely able in one field are quite hopeless in others. The best documented and most researched kind of ability is that of intelligence, although the concept is still clouded in some uncertainty. The work of Professor P. E. Vernon is extremely helpful in this respect. Vernon talks of three uses of the word 'intelligence', referring to them as intelligence A, B and C.

Intelligence A is an innate capacity, inherited genetically by a child, which determines his capacity for learning. The problem about intelligence A is that we have to assume its existence although we can never actually measure it.

Intelligence B is closer to the commonly accepted sense of 'he is an intelligent person'. A child is thought to be intelligent if he is good at understanding, reasoning, seeing relationships and is generally 'mentally efficient'.

Finally, Intelligence C is what we can measure by means of intelligence tests.[7] If it is a good test C will give us a good indication of B, but not necessarily of A. Why not? The reason for this discrepancy is that Intelligence A is defined in terms of pure innate ability — derived from the genes. Intelligence B is, however, the result of the inter-action of Intelligence A with the social and physical environment. Intelligence C is no more than a sample of skills and it is a partial, but sometimes very useful, view of a child's ability.

It is clear, therefore, that if someone achieves a low score on an intelligence test, this *may* mean that he is not very intelligent (A), but it may mean that he has not been exposed to the most favourable environment (including school environment). It may also mean the test did not give an adequate opportunity for the pupil to display his real ability. Many studies have shown, for example, that tests are not really 'fair' to working-class children in Britain or to Black children in some parts of the USA.

It would, therefore, always be safer to assume that people are capable of improvement. It is always possible that Intelligence C is an underestimate of Intelligence B or A. Acting on this assumption is much safer for teachers than simply assuming that a pupil is 'stupid'. In Chapter 1 it was noted that Professor Vernon concluded that about 5% of pupils were wrongly selected (partly by intelligence tests) for grammar or modern schools.

Intelligence tests may be used constructively in schools to make sure that pupils are not under-achieving, that is, failing to produce work up to their measured capacity. This is a positive use of intelligence tests and can be extremely beneficial as a means of diagnosis. However, tests have also sometimes been used negatively, that is, simply to label children as stupid and, therefore, not worth bothering with at least as far as difficult work is concerned. Teachers should bear two points in mind: first, that tests are neither sufficiently accurate nor sufficiently close to Intelligence A to be relied upon in this respect; second, that a teacher's task is to teach pupils of all abilities. Simply because a child has a low score on an IQ test is not an excuse for him to be labelled as less worthy of educational treatment. The teacher's professional responsibility is to find ways of helping children to learn who do not find the learning task easy.

Language

One of the most important skills for a teacher in encouraging learning is the ability to manipulate language. This includes the teacher's own ability to use language appropriately, and also the ability to encourage children to develop their language competence. An unfortunate feature about the debate on language in recent years has been the tendency to over-simplify research findings. The result has been the loose usage of such phrases as 'linguistically deprived' or 'culturally deprived', and to explain educational failure simply as the result of that kind of supposed deprivation. No child can be culturally deprived unless he is one of a very small number who get shut away from companionship altogether — that is, deprived of the culture of other human beings. These children's difficulties are quite different from the problems of the majority of children in our schools. Working-class children, for example, are part of a culture, but this culture is different from most teachers' culture. Similarly, the term 'linguistically deprived' is nearly always used inappropriately. Very few children are without language, but their language may be different from the language of the school.

Nevertheless, there remains the problem of being able to encourage children whose language does not equip them adequately for schools as they are at present organised. The research of Basil Bernstein and his colleagues indicates that there are important linguistic differences in our society between working-class children and middle-class children. We should however be very careful about using such terms as inferior and superior. It is certainly true that in many of our primary and secondary schools most working-class children find some difficulties of adjustment. It is the teacher's responsibility to enable children to make this adjustment rather than to write them off as educational failures.

There is now a good deal of research evidence available which would be helpful to teachers in the classroom. Joan Tough (1973), for example, shows that teachers need to learn to be sensitive to a child's willingness to be drawn into conversation. Probing or further questioning by the teacher when the child feels insecure will merely discourage him from further spontaneous speech. Joan Tough gives many illustrations of how this kind of problem should be tackled. Barnes and his co-authors (1969) have done a good deal of interesting work in secondary schools. They show, for instance, that teachers often overlook or underrate what children have to say by insisting on the 'language of the secondary school'. One interesting example is the extract from a chemistry lesson where an experiment about the suspension of solids in liquid lapsed into everyday language and the pupils started talking about milk turning to cheese, and smelling like cheese; instead of taking advantage of that link between school and reality, the teacher pushed the pupils on to the next topic and retreated once again into technical language.

Another important point which emerges from Barnes' research is that teachers not only talk too much, but when they do ask questions indulge in 'closed' questions when only one answer is expected. Barnes advocates much greater use of open-ended questions which would allow children to explore their own ideas and come to a variety of possible solutions. In the same book (Barnes 1969) Rosen labels this kind of teaching as 'getting the pupils to tell the teacher what they know he already knows'.

What much of this research amounts to is that teachers should know more about language processes (but not necessarily complicated linguistic theories) and be trained to practise these skills in the classroom. The idea of 'language across the curriculum' which was put forward by Barnes in 1969 was taken up in the Bullock Report[8] as the need for all schools to develop a policy for language across the curriculum. Unfortunately, the attempts to put this policy into practice have not so far met with any great success. This would appear to be one of those areas where the basic research work has been done, but its implementation in schools has yet to be achieved. Probably a good deal more in-service education for teachers is required on this topic.

Summary

One of the most neglected aspects of teaching and learning is the art of structuring subject-matter. Two kinds of structuring can be distinguished: identifying and making clear the 'logic of the disciplines'; selecting content in terms of the appropriate stage of development, background and ability of individual pupils. Teachers need to know more about cognitive development and intelligence, not least so that they are not misled by over-simplified versions of some theories.

NOTES

1 **One of the examples** of educational jargon which should be noted at this stage is the distinction often made between process and product — that is, it is the process of learning (and learning to learn) which is important rather than the product, that is, the knowledge stored away in the mind at the end. This is misleading for two reasons: first, some knowledge is important for its own sake; second, in some subjects the process is the product, for example, reading a poem. In some respects, the distinction is still a useful one, and the general tendency to focus on process rather than product is healthy provided that it does not go to extremes.

2 **Other aspects of 'discovery learning'** are dealt with in Chapter 8 as well as in some other sections of this book. An important book in this area is *Psychology: A Cognitive View* (Ausubel 1968).

3 **There is an important point** to be made here about the nature of knowledge and the nature of the learning process. The two are distinct, though overlapping. An essential aspect of a subject or a discipline is that it has a structure of concepts and sets of procedures. It is important for teachers to know their subject in this way, but it is also important for them to know how children learn. Questions of 'sequence' may be partly concerned with the logic of the discipline, but partly with the process of children's learning; teachers may wish to work from the concrete to the abstract and allow this to override part of the logic of the discipline. In that respect, the process of learning would have to take priority over the structure of the subject, but not, it is hoped, too drastically.

4 **Piaget's Stages of Development:**

Stage 1 — sensori-motor (0 to 2 years approximately) During the sensori-motor stage the child learns to co-ordinate perceptual and motor functions and to utilise certain elementary schemata for dealing with external objects. The child learns that objects exist even when outside the perceptual field, and he gradually co-ordinates their parts into a whole which is recognisable from different perspectives. This is regarded essentially as the pre-symbolic stage, but even so, during the second year elementary forms of symbolic behaviour begin to appear.

State 2 — pre-operational (2 to 7 years approximately) This state is characterised by the beginnings of organised symbolic behaviour — language in particular. The child is now representing the external world by internalising elementary forms of symbolism, but he is completely limited to his direct immediate experiences and lacks the ability to relate these experiences to similar past or future situations.

State 3 — concrete operations (7 to 11 years approximately) This stage is reached at about seven, and the child will by now have enlarged his ability to organise means independently of the immediate goal. He will have acquired the concepts of conservation and reversibility, and will have extended his use of symbols to assimilate past and present experience to future situations.

Stage 4 — formal operations (12 to 15 years approximately) This stage will involve development of the ability to use hypothetical reasoning based on the logic of all possible combinations and to perform controlled experimentation. But note the qualifications made in the discussion of the theories of Professor Peel (pages 53-4).

5 **Schema** (plural, *schemata*) is a term which Piaget borrowed from the philosopher Kant. A schema is the process of making sense of unique perceptions by putting them into a category.

6 **Bruner's book** *Toward a Theory of Instruction* (1966) — see bibliography — is particularly relevant in this respect.

7 **Intelligence tests** are sometimes used to arrive at a child's intelligence quotient (IQ). If a child is exactly average for his age, he will have an IQ of 100; if he is below average in the test he will be given an IQ of less than 100; and if he is above average for his age, his IQ will be more than 100.

IQ is worked out in a very simple way. If a child can solve problems which on average are typical of older children, he is said to have a *mental* age higher than his actual or chronological age. For example, if a boy of 10 could answer questions more like the average 12 year old, he would be said to have a mental age of 12, and an IQ of 120. The exact MA (mental age) is worked out carefully by the test results, and the exact IQ is then worked out by the following formula:

$$\frac{\text{Mental Age (MA)}}{\text{Chronological Age (CA)}} \times 100 = \text{IQ}$$

Using the same example as before,

MA = 12, CA = 10

$$\frac{12}{10} \times 100 = 120$$

8 **A Language for Life (1975)** Report of the Committee of Enquiry appointed by the Secretary of State for Education and Science (The Bullock Report).

The Bullock Committee was set up mainly to enquire into the teaching of reading in schools at a time when 'standards' were in question. But the Committee interpreted its brief very widely as 'Language in Education' on the principle that reading, writing, talking and listening should be treated as a unity. All schools were urged to develop a policy for 'Language across the Curriculum'.

4 The School as an Organisation for Teaching and Learning

In Chapter 1 we saw how the tradition developed in the UK that there should be a system of free education for all young people to enable them to become autonomous[1] individuals in a democratic, industrial society. Chapter 2 took this principle, applied it to the content of education, and discussed the kind of curriculum which would be suitable for those purposes; Chapter 3 looked at some of the psychological processes involved in the kind of teaching and learning which would be necessary to produce that kind of person.

A good deal of emphasis has therefore been placed on freedom: one of the functions of the school is to prepare young people to be 'free' (and responsible) in a free society. It has sometimes seemed ironic that in order to produce freedom we *compel* young people to spend ten or eleven years in institutions called schools. This apparent contradiction has been so acute for some educationists that they have despaired of schools altogether, and emphasised the contrast between 'schooling' and 'education'. Some of these 'deschoolers',[2] such as John Holt, have concentrated on the evils of traditional, authoritarian schools which dehumanise individuals rather than prepare them for human freedom; others, such as Ivan Illich, concentrate on education as one of many institutions (including medicine) used by the state to oppress individuals into conformity.

One of the questions we have to ask is whether it is possible for compulsory institutions to encourage individuals towards greater freedom. There are a number of problems in this which will need to be clarified.

There is another way of approaching this problem which may be helpful in removing some misconceptions about the nature of schools. In our society we value freedom so highly that we often try to pretend it exists even when it does not, and perhaps could not. Sociologists have made a useful distinction between voluntary and involuntary associations, In a voluntary association, such as a club or a debating society, people belong because they want to; they not only consent to membership but they probably also have to apply and be vetted by other members. Involuntary associations, such as prisons or a conscript army, are quite different: 'membership' is compulsory. Now on that one major criterion schools are involuntary and are more like prisons than youth clubs; but many teachers would prefer schools to be as little like prisons as possible, acting on the assumption or belief that if the aim of education is autonomy, then freedom within the institution is important. Other teachers would prefer schools to be unlike prisons simply because they do not care for working in a prison-like atmosphere. Yet other teachers, believing their role to be to enforce conformity, might be more comfortable in the role of disciplinarian or warder. One of the reasons why educationists such as John Holt have criticised schools is precisely because there is a strong tradition of the drill sergeant schoolteacher. [3]

But trying to make schools free even when they are compulsory may lead to a number of difficulties: for example, in secondary schools choice is usually built into the option system for fourteen year old pupils, although it has often been pointed out that the basis of this choice is frequently ill-founded or even irrational. It has sometimes also been suggested that what exists in such schools is not free choice, but a system of apparent freedom and actual manipulation. [4] Perhaps it would be better to recognise the compulsory nature of schools, but to maximise real rationality with those necessary constraints.

The major question then becomes: what kind of institution should we try to encourage schools to be? Schools cannot be completely free if attendance is compulsory (and expulsion difficult). But even without that constraint we would have to ask how much freedom within a school is desirable. Because a society wishes to have free adults, it does not necessarily imply that the immature young should also be completely free, although they need to learn how to become free and to live in a free society. This problem is related to what has sometimes been referred to as the 'paradox of moral education': the final aim of moral education is to produce a morally autonomous individual (that is, someone who not only does the right things but does them for the right reasons, acting rationally and freely). To produce that kind of individual, however, it may be necessary to instill good moral habits in very young children, long before they can understand the purpose behind the habits or rules being encouraged. It is possible that this paradox extends to other kinds of education as well as moral.

A closely related problem to that of the kind of organisation schools ought to be, is the kind of professional behaviour which we should expect from teachers. To what extent must they be authority figures? To what extent must they insist as well as persuade? A good deal has been written in books about the sociology of education on the role of the teacher, but not all of it is of very much help to the young teacher in the classroom. Some research has shown that it is this dilemma about exerting authority which above all others makes inexperienced teachers anxious. Hannam, Smyth and Stephenson (1971) have given some graphic illustrations of the difficulties faced by young student teachers in their work in Bristol.[5] Many young teachers feel that they do not want to 'boss children about'; they want to be pleasant and helpful, and they feel very uncomfortable if they have to punish or even reprimand, yet the school situation appears to make it necessary to do all of these things.

I want to suggest that although 'child centred' approaches to education were a welcome and much needed reaction against Victorian harshness (just as Rousseau was reacting in a similar way against seventeenth-century attitudes to children), they do not represent a realistic formula for organising schools or prescribing the behaviour of teachers today. We can accept as a general hypothesis the idea of a child being natually curious, wanting to learn and being eager to co-operate with others, without accepting completely the idea of a school without any rules, with no limits on individual freedom and without any need for 'work' in the form of a curriculum. We can also accept the idea of a teacher who wants to be a benevolent friend rather than a harsh disciplinarian without denying the need for order in schools and the exercise of authority by teachers.

Educational Theories

On what basis can a formula for well organised schools and professional teachers be devised and justified? In order to answer that question we must venture a little into the world of education theory. T.W. Moore (1974)[6] has suggested that an educational theory tries to give 'comprehensive, over-arching guidance in the conduct of education . . . usually associated with a distinctive, social and political position' (pp. 8-9). An educational theory is, therefore, essentially prescriptive, unlike scientific theory, as well as being descriptive. Any of the well-known theorists of education — Plato or Rousseau — had a particular social or political axe to grind. Any theory that I put forward in this book will reflect my own social and political values, but it would be a waste of time writing about them unless I was convinced that these values were shared by a sizeable proportion of the teachers and other members of our democratic society today. We cannot hope to have complete consensus, but we must work on the assumption that a good deal of agreement on a number of major issues is both desirable and possible.

T.W. Moore suggests that any general educational theory must rest on three kinds of value judgments: first, assumptions about those who are to be educated — human beings and especially children; second, assumptions about the purpose or aims of education; and third, assumptions about the nature of knowledge, especially the worthwhile values of certain kinds of knowledge. These assumptions would be related to other assumptions about how knowledge is acquired and how it is learned and should be taught (I have already discussed some of these assumptions in Chapters 2 and 3 of this book).

The Utilitarian Theory

One of the problems about educational theory in England is that teachers often claim to reject it. They prefer to see themselves as good practitioners for whom theory is irrelevant. But engaging in an activity like teaching is impossible without some underlying theory or set of assumptions, or values, just as it is impossible to be a doctor without having some underlying theory of good health. When a teacher claims to be operating without any theory, he is probably using a second-hand theory without realising it. In England probably the most influential educational theory today is a hangover from nineteenth-century Utilitarianism and the writings of Jeremy Bentham, James Mill, and the latter's son John Stuart Mill. Many teachers are still working on the theory set out by James Mill[7] (1821) which rests upon the following assumptions:

About the nature of man

Human beings are essentially selfish. People (including children) act only to increase pleasure or to avoid pain. The minds of human beings at birth are empty. They are like clean slates or empty rooms gradually to be filled up with the furniture provided by experiences from sensations derived from their environment. The teachers' job is to fill children up with useful information.

About aims (including assumptions about the educated man)

The purpose of all rational activity, including education, is to increase happiness and to diminish pain. The particular aim of education is to produce the kind of people whose behaviour will increase not only their own happiness but also that of other human beings. The educated person would, therefore, have virtues such as temperance, generosity and justice, and would also have a good deal of useful knowledge and sagacity (the ability to use knowledge wisely).

About knowledge and teaching

Connected with the *tabula rasa* or clean slate theory of the mind is the doctrine that ideas tend to associate together according to the frequency with which elements in the environment are experienced together. (For example, fire and heat are natural connections, but teachers will also try to build up connections between stealing and punishment, and so on.) Education consists in forming desirable trains of ideas in pupils' minds. The curriculum should, therefore, consist of planned associations of the 'natural' kind as well as the 'artificial' — science and mathematics as well as history, literature, philosophy and religion. The most effective teaching method would systematically join certain sensations and ideas in the pupils' mind by presenting them frequently and in the context of pleasure.

It may be that this Utilitarian theory is still the dominant teaching theory for most secondary school teachers. Others will share the dominant educational theory of primary school teachers (and especially infant teachers) which is a child-centred theory derived from Rousseau. This states that human beings (especially children before they have been corrupted by society) are essentially good and co-operative. The purpose of education is to protect them from an evil corrupting society, and to allow them to develop 'naturally'. The best method of allowing children to become educated is to enable them to follow their own interests and merely to assist them, without interfering too much in their naturally developing maturity.

A Reformulated Theory

If teachers in a school are knowingly or unknowingly following either of those two educational 'theories', then the school will need to come to terms with this situation and plan accordingly. Probably, most teachers will not be totally committed to either of those two ideologies, but will be following a set of principles somewhere in the middle of those two extremes. It might help, therefore, if a school can establish its own twentieth-century educational theory which might be something like the following:

Assumptions about human nature

People are not essentially selfish, nor are they essentially good. They are a mixture of potentialities which are both good and evil. Children are naturally curious, and they want to learn. But curiosity will not necessarily carry them all the way that is necessary in a modern complex society. There will still be a need to develop some of the Utilitarian values such as hard work, perseverance, and so on. Men and women are essentially social beings. This should be reflected in what is learnt and how it is learnt. All can benefit from education; no one is completely ineducable. Some will learn more than others, or more quickly than others, but this is essentially a difference in degree rather than a difference in kind. Schools should look for similarities between human beings as well as differences. In a democratic society it is important to recognise the essential humanity and communality of all human beings.

Assumptions about aims (education is concerned with improving or developing pupils in some way)

In a democratic society it is necessary for individuals to become autonomous: that is, to be able to make decisions for themselves over a wide range of activities rather than simply to follow orders, or to be conformists. The aim will be to produce not simply autonomous individuals, but autonomous individuals living in a society, knowing their duties and responsibilities as well as rights and privileges. The educated person in a democratic society should be a co-operative individual not a selfish individualist. The aim of education will be to introduce all members of society to the common culture of that society. It will not be enough to succeed with a small minority of pupils, and it will not be satisfactory to have a different kind of education for different social or intellectual levels. Social justice in education must mean equality of access to worthwhile knowledge and experience (while accepting and welcoming different levels of achievement in different kinds of knowledge).

Assumptions about knowledge and learning

The school must have a policy or a working plan about the structure of knowledge. It must also be possible to justify why the school values some kinds of knowledge more highly than others (see Chapter 7).

Such a programe is in no way in conflict with legislation and central recommendations about education since 1944. As we saw in Chapter 1, the 1944 Education Act laid down the foundation for this kind of democratic approach to education which has been filled out by successive circulars and recommendations such as the 1977 Green Paper on education, as well as by the documents produced by HMI.[8] It would not be accepted by the whole population of this country or even by all teachers, but it would probably be accepted by a majority.

What kind of school would be required to put into operation such a theory or programme? The first requirement is that a school should be orderly and purposeful: if the state is going to deprive the young of eleven years of their 'freedom' (or idleness), then it has a duty to provide an environment which is safe and where the benefits are clear. The benefits should be clear not only to the teachers, but, in so far as it is possible, to the pupils as well. It will not always be possible to explain to pupils (especially the very young) why certain kinds of learning experiences are thought to be worthwhile or necessary, but that should not be used as an excuse for not trying. Discipline, control, or good order are also essential in a school as in any other community. It may be a mistake to think that co-operativeness and concern for others simply develops — it may be necessary for teachers to foster this development and to insist on rules being observed. This kind of insistence may be necessary for two reasons. The first is because, unless we have accepted the doctrine of total innate goodness, then individual children will from time to time behave selfishly, unco-operatively, or even with cruelty, and they must be stopped both for their own education and for the smooth running of the whole community. To take an easy, uncontroversial example to make the case: if a large boy bullies a smaller one, then the small boy has a right of protection; the larger one needs to be corrected. It is the teacher's job both to protect and correct; it is the function of a good school to enable him to do it. The second reason concerns the fact that children in groups do not always behave in the way they would as individuals: once again they must be controlled and educated. All communities and institutions such as clubs have rules, why should schools be an exception? If the school as a community has no clear rules, or if teachers do not implement them, then the pupils themselves will impose a system of norms which may not be educationally acceptable.

In order to justify schools, we have to make an assumption that children will benefit from attending these schools, and that the teachers have something to offer children which the children could not work out or discover for themselves. These offerings are of at least two kinds: values and knowledge. In each case the argument is similar, but it may be easier to see the case for the transmission of knowledge. In Chapter 2, the case was argued for children developing an understanding of science: if pupils were left to discover science entirely on their own they would learn very little: it is the teacher's task to look at the scientific discoveries of previous generations, structure the subject matter in a way which will provide a short-cut for pupils, and present it to them. To do this, the teacher must know his science and his pupils. A similar argument could be developed for moral values: left to themselves there is no guarantee the pupils would develop a moral code any less primitive than the science that they might invent. (*Lord of the Flies* makes interesting reading in this respect.)

What all this amounts to is that if schools are provided in order to facilitate the transmission of knowledge and values, then teachers have to be invested with the necessary authority to perform this task efficiently. In this context it is very important to distinguish between authority and authoritarianism. An authoritarian teacher is one who expects obedience for its own sake and without any questioning by the pupils. This would be an essentially irrational and anti-educational process, but that is not to say that the exercise of authority comes into the same category.

Authority

The question of authority, order and control is of great interest to sociologists, and this is one area where the writings of academic sociologists may have some relevance to the teacher in the classroom. Sociologists are interested in such questions as why people do as they are told. One of the major sociologists to write about authority was the German theorist, Max Weber (1864-1920). Weber suggested that there were three kinds of authority (or three kinds of legitimation of authority): traditional authority, rational/legal authority, and charismatic authority.

Traditional authority

In the case of traditional authority, the authority of some is accepted by others because it has been regarded as valid, perhaps even unquestionable, for a long time. We have always obeyed that kind of person — perhaps a king, or a baron, or a chief. It is a non-controversial acceptance of authority, accompanied by a vague feeling that it would be wrong even to doubt the legitimacy of the authority. Quite clearly in the past this kind of authority was one which prevailed in our society generally, not only in education, but there has been a move away from it in political and work situations, and people now question whether anyone has the right to make certain demands and issue orders. In England, the medieval king could exercise arbitrary authority, limited only by the framework of custom. For example, the arguments in the sixteenth and seventeenth centuries about the right of the king to impose certain kinds of taxes were not questions about whether or not the imposition was fair or reasonable, but whether or not it was customary.

Legal/rational authority

This mode of legitimation of power exists where there are good reasons for accepting the authority. Authority in this case is part of an institution which is in some way beneficial to those receiving the orders. It is in accord with some more general rule such as fairness or justice. A judge has the legal and moral right to imprison individuals, for the public good, but private persons in the same country have no such authority to restrict liberty in that way.

Charismatic authority

This kind of authority is associated with individuals possessing charisma. Charismatic individuals might include very different people such as Christ, Napoleon and Hitler. The authority depends on a belief that the wielder of authority has sacred or superhuman qualities. His followers are disciples. Charisma can, however, be transmitted institutionally: for example, in the ordination of priests. In that case the principle might be that the office is more important than the individual. There may be elements of this in the role of the teacher — the idea of wearing a gown, cultivating superior manners, or aloof and haughty behaviour. To some extent,this kind of charisma can be taught, though not to everyone. Candidates for charismatic authority training have to be selected carefully and their success depends less on knowledge than on their demeanour.

Weber's typology is interesting and useful, and obviously has some relevance to the behaviour of teachers. Two qualifications need to be made, however. The first is that some people have misused this classification and talked of 'charismatic personality' sometimes in connection with teachers, but this is really a misuse of the sociological term. Second, the Weberian view is not accepted by all sociologists.[10]

I should like to leave aside the question of charismatic authority for the moment and concentrate on the other two aspects — traditional and legal/rational. It is, of course, important to bear in mind that Weber described these three kinds of authority as 'ideal types', that is, not existing in their pure form but useful for guiding and thinking through our classification. If we accept the Weberian typology, what seems to have been happening in society as a whole, and more recently in schools, is that there has been a marked shift from traditional authority to legal/rational authority. Pupils in schools are also less willing to accept the authority of the school or of individual teachers simply because teachers have always been obeyed. Teachers now have to justify authority in rational terms. The authority of teachers is put in the balance against the rights of pupils.

The change in attitude to authority is also seen in regard to school rules. In the past rules might have been obeyed (or disobeyed), but the basis of the rules was not necessarily called into question — they were there simply as school rules. Today, pupils certainly ask and sometimes demand answers to such questions as 'Why should we learn French?' 'Why should we wear school uniforms?' 'Why are we not allowed to wear jewellery?' Some schools have tackled this problem by attempting to make the school itself more rational, and the authority relationship between staff and pupils is completely rational. Other schools have sometimes successfully resisted the pressure and maintained a traditional authority — 'Do as you are told because I tell you', or, 'Don't ask questions like that.' Perhaps the majority of schools, however, have moved somewhere away from the really effective situation of completely traditional authority without ever reaching a totally rational basis of authority. Teachers in many schools find themselves in a marginal position where they are expected to maintain and enforce irrational rules without even the traditional backing of the school as an institution. This is a difficult position for teachers, sometimes it becomes impossible.

The teacher may find himself in an extremely delicate relationship with pupils. He is entrusted with the care of young people and expected to guide and mould them. Yet his authority is increasingly called into question. Some teachers even feel uneasy about using authority at all. An additional complication is that the teacher's role involves making himself redundant as soon as possible: if a teacher is successful he must enable the pupil to be capable of educating himself — to cease to need the teacher. The paradoxical situation for the teacher is that the more successful he is as a teacher, the less right he has to impose his authority on the pupil.

One further distinction needs to be made: authority is not the same as competence and it is not the same as leadership. R.S. Peters[11] has made an interesting distinction between a teacher being *in* authority and being *an* authority. A person in authority does not have to possess competence (to be *an* authority). The authority figure is simply given a certain status in order to preserve order: for example, a policeman does not have to be particularly good at directing the traffic, but he has authority which motorists do not; a treasurer does not have to be good at signing cheques, but he has authority to do so. The teacher is in authority to preserve good order, and to enable the school to function, but he is also an authority in the sense of being more knowledgeable than the pupils. He has to be an expert and he has also to be given certain powers by the authorities of the school. This is a useful distinction, but it is made more complicated by the fact that authority of some kinds does depend to some extent on competence. A football referee needs to know the rules otherwise his authority will be questioned by the players and by the spectators; teachers must be authorities on the knowledge they are transmitting and also be able to communicate successfully, otherwise their position in authority will be questioned by the pupils.

Teachers should, therefore, not feel uncomfortable about their authority. They should be prepared to exercise it provided that they are confident that they have some worthwhile knowledge to offer to their pupils, and provided that their position in authority is exercised rationally rather than arbitrarily. If teachers are satisfied on both of those counts, then they should have no qualms about exercising their authority and should concentrate simply on how to do it successfully. It is clear from this discussion of authority that the exercise of authority in school is not simply a matter for the individual teacher, but is a question of the organisation as a whole. Individual teachers should not be left to their own devices: there should be some institutional framework which provides a suitable back-up to the teacher's individual authority, especially if it is questioned or opposed. It is precisely this which appears to be lacking in many schools. The problem has been made more acute by the fact that, with the development of comprehensive schools, schools have tended to become much larger. Whereas the authority arrangements in a small grammar school could be dealt with on an informal basis, in a larger school (perhaps three times as large) the arrangements have to be formalised and institutionalised.

Classroom Control

However good a teacher's lesson preparation and planning may be, he is likely to encounter one or two pupils in a class who will be disruptive and spoil the lesson for the rest of the pupils. He must have some means of dealing with those pupils in order to make life tolerable for the rest of the class as well as for himself. There needs to be some method of removing children from that class either temporarily or on permanent basis. Some schools have now developed a variety of means of coping with 'disruptive' pupils: this may be in the form of a temporary 'sanctuary', or a more permanent unit inside or attached to a school. In particularly difficult cases it may be better to have totally separate arrangements made for the education of a tiny minority of the pupils.

One of the more disturbing features of the development of large comprehensive schools in the UK has been the lack of attention given to research which has already been done elsewhere on the size of schools.[12] Lessons learnt about education in the USA can never be transferred automatically to another country, but some attention should have been paid to research which showed that in many respects small schools have considerable advantages over larger organisations, especially as regards involvement and participation of the pupils, motivation and school spirit. Even some of the supposed advantages of large schools (for example, wider choice of subjects) are often more apparent than real.

In those cases where we already have large schools, what is necessary is to examine very carefully the various ways that have been tried for sub-dividing large educational institutions into smaller units and less anonymous groups. The traditional means of achieving that was to split the school into vertical house systems. This was very popular in grammar schools and was taken over by larger comprehensive schools, but has sometimes not worked in pratice. A feature of house organisations in comprehensive schools is the tutor group rather than the form as the basic unit. The tutor group is a unit of about twenty pupils deliberately mixed as regards age and ability under the guidance of a tutor group teacher, who remains with that group for a number of years. The housemaster or mistress in charge of a house (perhaps ten tutor groups) will try to know all the members individually and devote some time to pastoral or counselling duties. Assemblies, lunch, games and other activities may be organised on a house basis.

Some research has shown (Benn and Simon 1968) that house systems sometimes operate to maximum advantage only when the school has been purpose-built for house organisations. During the last fifteen years, horizontal year grouping has become more popular. Every pupil will be well known by his form teacher, slightly less well known but still identifiable by a year group leader. The head will not necessarily know the name of every pupil, but will know how to find it out. What is clear is that some means of breaking down large schools into smaller social units is absolutely essential. Small is not necessarily beautiful in all respects, but anonymous is certainly unhelpful in an educational context.[13]

Finally, we come to the question of classroom management. Ultimately it is the teacher's job to be as effective as possible in his own classroom. Classroom management is not something which can be dealt with in a few paragraphs, but a few general principles may be outlined. (*See* Robertson[14] (1981) for a very comprehensive treatment of the problem of classroom management.) Classroom management may be divided into two interrelated categories: lesson planning, and classroom control.

Lesson planning is, essentially, to translate into individual lesson terms the kind of principles which were discussed in Chapter 3. There is, for example, a good deal of research evidence which shows that the most widespread fault in teaching is for teachers to talk too much. While not accepting the principle that children need to discover everything for themselves, it is certainly true that simply lecturing children is a most ineffective way of enabling them to learn. They need to be active in some way, rather than simply passively accepting the information or views provided by the teacher.

Another important feature of most classes is that teachers do not sufficiently cater for different levels of ability. There is a tendency to teach to the middle and let the brighter ones get bored and the slower ones get lost or fall further behind. This problem is partly solved by teachers not relying on their own spoken words to such a great extent, but even if materials are provided it is important that these should be provided at a variety of levels. This point relates Chapter 2 to Chapter 3: there should be, in a common curriculum, a variety of entrances and exits for different pupils. A possible plan would be as follows: first, the teacher should make a selection of topics or questions to be explored, or generalisations to be encouraged, to which pupils should be exposed by the end of a teaching session (perhaps a term, or a year, or even longer). This selection should be derived from the basic structure of the discipline and the most important content to be covered.

The next step is to arrange these topics in a sequence. For each basic core topic, the teacher must work out additional topics or themes at a variety of levels of difficulty, which also cater for a variety of individual interests. Some pupils will spend most, but not all, of their time on the basic topics while others will be reaching greater levels of depth in a particular area. It should not be assumed that those who cover most ground are necessarily the most able. Some children work quickly, but superficially. It is an important aspect of the teacher's role to ensure that sufficient basic learning is taking place.

It is important to bear in mind that pupils differ not only in levels of ability but also in learning styles. The structure of a discipline and its sequence may be regarded as fixed, but it is the responsibility of the teacher to match individual pupils' learning styles with the particular tasks in hand. This is by no means easy, but it is a mark of the professional teacher that he can cope with this problem. To some extent, it will be simply a matter of trial and error, once having prepared a variety of approaches. What it amounts to, however, is that a pupil who 'fails' is not simply regarded as incapable of tackling that particular kind of work, but is provided with an alternative approach to the concept or material. The teacher's role in this respect is essentially that of mediator between the knowledge and the individual pupil. The curriculum is common in the sense that it must be available to all pupils, but the appraoch to it is not a single channel.

This approach has sometimes been referred to in the USA as 'mastery learning'.[15] Benjamin Bloom has criticised the teaching profession for its low expectations of pupils. Bloom suggests that most teachers expect about a third of pupils to fail, or just 'get by'. They expect another third to learn a good deal of what they have to teach but not enough to be regarded as good students. This leaves a third who are regarded as satisfactory students. Surely this is an unsatisfactory basis for planning? But it is an extremely common one in both the USA and UK. Bloom suggests that most students – perhaps more than 90% – are capable of mastering what we want to teach them. One of the major problems in most clasrooms is that far too many pupils fail and begin to regard themselves as failures. It is not disputed that pupils have different aptitudes for various subjects, but we have to ask whether low aptitude simply excuses a teacher for failing to teach. Bloom accepts Carroll's (1963) view that 'aptitude is the amount of time required by the learner to attain mastery of a learning task'. The classroom disease diagnosed by Carroll is that despite differences in aptitude, the usual practice in schools is to provide all pupils with roughly the same kind and amount of instruction. The solution is clear: for pupils with lower aptitude in a specific area of the curriculum, more time should be spent, but not simply more of the same kind of instruction — different approaches and teaching techniques will be essential to prevent boredom and rebellion.

Bloom (1971) quotes the unpublished research by Dave (1963) to show that for some pupils on a mathematics course, the correlation between low mathematical aptitude and the year examination results was zero. For middle-class pupils, poor ability was adequately compensated for by individual tutoring at home. For those who received no help outside the classroom, the correlation between aptitude and achievement was zero. The key variable seemed to be the willingness of the pupil to persist, which was related to the appropriateness of the instruction rather than the simple amount of time spent. The major factor in all this is that pupils should not regard themselves as failing: if the teacher gives them work appropriate to their level of ability and progress, then a certain amount of positive feedback should enable the pupils to see themselves in a success role. In order to achieve this, teachers will have to learn to keep much better records and to make use of better materials.

Finally, we come to the second aspect of classroom management: individual teacher control of pupils and the class as a whole. Once again, teachers create a good deal of trouble for themselves by talking too much, as was suggested above. Related to this is the fact that most teachers do not expect enough work from most pupils, and do not demand enough. This is not to suggest that we go back to the nineteenth-century Gradgrind approach to teaching, simply that one golden rule for every school and for every teacher should be not to waste any pupil's time. An analysis of the average lesson makes it clear that far too much time is wasted. Not only do pupils get bored, but they use up their energy in illicit ways. Much more should be expected and much more demanded of pupils in every classroom. Far from making it necessary to impose an iron discipline to achieve the objecives, classroom control will then become much easier when there is plenty of work for everyone to be doing. A teacher needs to dominate the classroom, but this does not mean that he has to be domineering or authoritarian (Robertson 1981).

Summary

Many teachers are so uncomfortable about the use of authority that their effectiveness in the classroom is impaired. At the other extreme, some teachers remain authoritarian at a time when such behaviour is generally deplored. The rightful use of authority has been examined. Teachers need to have something worthwhile to teach and be able to dominate the classroom in order to succeed.

NOTES

1 **Autonomous.** This is a concept not without problems in education. The idea behind it is that of the person (child or adult) who not only does the right thing, but does it for the right reason: an autonomous person is self-directing in a rational way, not simple responding to orders or conforming to conventions.

2 **John Holt** began by being a reformer with his book *How Children Fail* (1964), but in his more recent *Freedom and Beyond* (1972) he has now moved over to being a complete de-schooler, that is, wishing to abolish compulsory schooling and compulsory institutions altogether. Other books in this field include Paul Goodman *Compulsory Mis-education* (1962). Ivan Illich is the most famous deschooler and his book *Deschooling Society* (1971) has been very influential in both the USA and UK.

3 **There is, of course, a link** between Chapter 2 and the discussion of the belief that children are naturally good or naturally evil. If children are naturally good, then there will be no need for rules; if evil, then original sin must be stamped out by harsh discipline and an oppressive set of rules. Presumably, most teachers today believe that the truth lies somewhere in the middle, that is, that children are neither wholly good nor wholly evil, so that rules will be necessary, but not oppressive.

4 **A number of studies** have now been published criticising option schemes. A recent one is *A Charter for Choice* (Hurman 1979). This book shows that the option system is organisational rather than educational in origin and outcome. It is also related to the selection procedure rather than the free choice of pupils.

5 **Charles Hannam** and his colleagues at the Bristol University School of Education have been working with student teachers and adolescents in local comprehensive schools in informal out-of-school activities. An account of the Hillview project is contained in Hannam *et. al.* (1971).

6 **Some writers** have suggested that it is inappropriate to use the word 'theory' in connection with education, on the grounds that theory ought to be confined to scientific theory where there is a process of data collection and hypothesis testing. In education, theory is used in a very different way to mean a set of guiding principles. A senior lecturer in philosophy at the University of London Institute of Education, T. W. Moore, has written a very useful book clarifying this point and outlining what an educational theory would have to consist of (Moore 1974).

7 *See* Burston, W.H. (1969) *James Mill on Education* (Cambridge University Press) as well as the chapter on Mill in Moore (1974).

8 *Education in Schools: A Consultative Document* (the 1977 Green Paper) restated the responsibilities of central government and LEAs about curriculum planning. This was followed in 1980 by a document from HMI called *A View of the Curriculum.*

9 *Lord of the Flies,* a novel by William Golding, describes an air crash on an deserted island where the only survivors are a group of schoolboys. Their behaviour is more in line with Hobbes than with Rousseau.

10 **The American sociologist Bierstedt,** for example, suggests that Weber's category of charismatic authority is not really authority at all, but a kind of leadership. *See* Bierstedt (1967).

11 **R.S. Peters,** *Ethics and Education,* Chapter 9. A person may be said to be *an* authority on Norman churches if he is an expert on that subject; his authority derives from his knowledge. A traffic warden may be said to be *in* authority because he has been authorised to do a certain job by appropriate superiors; his authority derives from his position. A teacher should be both in authority as well as an authority:

he must be able to control and organise the class as well as have some expertise to offer.

12 For example, Barker and Gump (1964).

13 **Recent research by Michael Rutter** (1979) and his colleagues is particularly relevant here. This was the result of a longitudinal survey of children in Inner London secondary schools. The encouraging result of the survey was that schools did differ in their social environments and that these differences were systematically associated with varying rates of problems and progress among pupils. There are good schools and bad schools as well as good teachers and not so good teachers. In more successful schools, teachers were more likely to work together as a group, courses were planned and co-ordinated within departments, and there was a general consensus on school policy. In good schools it was also more likely that teachers' work would be looked at by senior staff, another aspect of the importance of having a school policy rather than leaving teachers to their own devices. In the better schools, lessons were more work-orientated, with teachers spending less time on dealing with children's behaviour or setting up equipment and more time on the subject-matter of the lessons. Lessons also tended to start more promptly, and teachers maintained contact with the whole group rather than with sub-groups within the class.

14 **Robertson's book** *Effective Classroom Control* (1981) gives invaluable advice to teachers about how to act in a classroom. This includes questions of posture, eye contact and how to convey authority, as well as a number of principles to observe in dealing with difficult situations. It is impossible to summarise this advice here.

15 **Mastery learning** *See* Bloom (1971).

5 The Nature of Education

In Chapter 4, I made a number of suggestions for improving schools, and attempted to establish some principles about the school as an organisation. In that chapter, a number of assumptions were made about the nature of education which should now be specified in detail. We may think that we know what we mean when we use the word 'education', but when we come to examine it, it is by no means unambiguous.

I have already made a distinction between education and schooling: by implication I have also contrasted education and instruction. This may be an appropriate point in this text to stop and define 'education' more clearly. Education is very difficult to define because the word 'education' is used in such a wide variety of ways. Oscar Wilde's statement that 'education is what begins when you leave school' is a cynical view point which may be helpful in distinguishing the difference between education and schooling, but does not get us any further in defining the essential meaning of 'education'.

Much of the work on clarifying the concept 'education' has been carried out by Professor Richard (R.S.) Peters, whose book *Ethics and Education* should be read by all teachers. The following sections owe a good deal to Richard Peters' thinking, but it is inevitably an inadequate summary of his very rich argument, and my own interpretation may even distort his position.

Richard Peters established a new approach to the Philosophy of Education by applying the methods of analytic philosophy to the field of education. Analytic philosophy rejects metaphysical speculation about the universe as a whole, and concentrates on piecemeal clarification of problems by analysing meaning. Metaphysical[1] philosophers had tended to take meaning for granted and assume that there was a clear communication of an idea by all key words, but for analytic philosophers language is a central concern.

Peters uses the techniques of analytic philosophy to clarify basic concepts such as education, teaching, training, instruction and indoctrination, as well as many others. It would be unfair to suggest that this is his only contribution, however. Peters develops an educational theory based on his central definition of education. This is a theory which refuses to see education in purely instrumental terms, that is, simply as a means to an end. In Chapter 4, I criticised the Utilitarian approach to education because it tended to do just that; latter-day Utilitarians tend to see education simply in terms of 'producing skilled manpower' or 'training citizens'. For Peters, unlike the Utilitarians, education has intrinsic value, that is, it is worthwhile in itself. His definition of education emphasises that education is worthwhile not because it produces something else which is of value, but because it is valuable itself, although it is always an unfinished process;

> ... to be educated is not to have arrived at a destination; it is to travel with a different view.

It will be easier to understand the analytic approach by examining the word 'education' in the way that Peters discusses it. Education is not a word to which a single precise meaning can be attached. It is not a word like 'running' which immediately conjures up a picture of a single kind of activity. You can run quickly or very quickly, but all running is of essentially the same kind. Not so education or educating: education is associated with learning, but no specific type of activity is required. In this respect, according to Peters, 'education' is like 'reform'. Reform is not associated with any particular process: people may be reformed by solitary confinement, or by reading the Bible, or by listening to a sermon. Similarly, people may be educated by reading books, by listening to lectures, by conversation with appropriate individuals. In each case, we think that the word 'reform' or 'education' is properly used if certain criteria are met.

One of the criteria that both words have in common is that something worthwhile should be achieved. Education and reform both necessarily involve some kind of improvement. It would make no sense at all to say, 'Prison has reformed him, but he is a worse villain than ever.' Nor would it be meaningful to say, 'He has been well educated at that school, but he has learnt nothing of value.' Some change has to take place, and it must be a change in the 'right' direction. Education involves learning, but not all learning is educational: Oliver Twist learned from Fagin and the Artful Dodger how to pick pockets, but that could not be described as 'education'; what he learned was not something which made him a better person. Oliver was *trained* as a pick pocket and given *instruction* in that art, but he was not being educated.

The last example should make it clear that value judgments are inevitable in talking about education defined in this way. If we say that someone is educated, it implies we *value* certain aspects of the process he has been through. It does not, of course, imply total approval of an individual's character or behaviour. It is quite possible to say, 'He is well educated, but eats like a pig'; or, 'He is well educated, but extremely selfish'; but it would not make sense to say, 'He is well educated but knows nothing.' I would like to turn away from Peters' argument at this stage and make a sociological rather than a philosophical point: one of the difficulties with a word like 'education' is that the value judgments involved are not necessarily 'pure' – some activities may be described as educational not because they improve a person but because they are approved by the 'right' people. Some activities may be described as educational for social reasons rather than for their intrinsic 'improving' value. We will have to return to that point later – it has been much discussed (and misunderstood) by some 'new wave' sociologists of education.[2]

Meanwhile, we should return to the question of the meaning of education. Education is concerned with transmitting something that is worthwhile, but Peters inserts an additional condition, namely, that the transmission must be carried out in a morally unobjectionable manner.[3] The person being educated must know what is happening to him and must accept the process rationally: learning, even of worthwhile content, would not be educational if it were imparted by using techniques involving cruelty, or by brainwashing or conditioning. This is perhaps a complicating factor which has not been sufficiently discussed by educationists; in recent years, there has been a good deal of theorizing about the 'hidden curriculum'[4] (or the 'paracurriculum'), but this is not often related to definitions of education. What do pupils learn, for example, from operating within a prefect system or a cadet corps? Are these educational even if pupils (and teachers) are unaware of what is being learned? Can education be confined to what is contained in the official (that is, open) curriculum? These are also difficult questions to which we shall return later. Meanwhile, it may be helpful to summarise the argument so far using Peters' own three criteria:

1 that education implies the transmission of what is worthwhile to those who become committed to it;
2 that education must involve knowledge and understanding, and some kind of cognitive perspective, which are not inert;
3 that education at least rules out some procedures of transmission, on the grounds that they lack wittingness and voluntariness.

(*Ethics and Education*, page 45)

The point made in 2 above about cognitive perspective is connected with a difference in meaning between education and training. According to Peters 'training' is applicable when (a) there is some specifiable type of performance to be mastered, (b) practice is required for this mastery, (c) little emphasis is placed on underlying principles. Training also has a wider application than that of a single skill. 'Training' may be used when any clear-cut specification has to be learned. For example, military training includes not only specific skills such as weapon training but also the inculcation of habits such as punctuality and tidiness. Now, according to Peters, a man might be a very highly trained scientist, but not be an educated man. There is an apparent contradiction here, because science is, as we shall see later, an excellent example of a worthwhile activity. But Peters would deny this scientist the adjective 'educated' if he could not see science in connection with anything else (that is, see 'its place in a coherent pattern of life'). To be educated, therefore, is much more than merely being well informed or well trained. The possession of worthwhile knowledge is a necessary condition for being educated, but not a sufficient one. The educated man must also be able to see underlying principles and perceive relationships.

Another important reason for spending time on the meanings of key words in education is that terms such as 'instruction' become entangled in doctrinal disputes between advocates of traditional and advocates of progressive education. Clarification of the meaning of the word may serve to get educationists out of entrenched positions, see exactly what is at issue, and perhaps even close the gap between the opponents. The problem with 'instruction' is that it is something regarded with favour by traditionalists, but is a dirty word for progressive educationists. Traditionalists like instruction because it has connotations of hard work (rather than play) of acquiring knowledge (rather than being creative). To the progressives, instruction is associated with pupils sitting quietly in rows, listening to a teacher who is feeding them with information they do not really understand and are not really interested in. [5] Peters examines those methods of teaching (or encouraging learning) practised by progressives, such as taking children out of the classroom to give them first-hand experience, and comes to the conclusion that these are, in fact, simply intelligent methods of instruction. The teacher has an agenda in his head of what should be learned and he manipulates pupils and the environment to ensure that it is learned, but in a way which is acceptable and enjoyable to the pupils. If this counts as teaching, why not as instruction? This seems to be getting close to hairsplitting, but there is an important distinction to be made between that kind of learning and teaching which relies on the teacher passing on information or skills (for example, dictated notes in a science lesson), and that kind of teaching which allows children to collect evidence for themselves, to come to their own conclusions, even to make 'discoveries'. It is not a black and white distinction – there is a considerable grey area in the middle.

The question is confused still further by the fact that good teachers will tend to use a mixture of techniques rather than rely on one or the other of the two extreme methods described above. But there are certain kinds of teaching activity which might be better referred to as 'instruction'. We learn to drive a car from a driving instructor, for example, (it might be an expensive business finding out how to drive by trial and error rather than by being told). In the army we have weapon-training instructors (not teachers). 'Instruction' is properly used when the matter to be learned is very clear-cut: where there is an unambiguous distinction between correct and incorrect information (the date of the Battle of Waterloo) or a right and a wrong way of performing a skill (cleaning a rifle). Dates in history can be learned by simple instruction, but not how to understand the nature of historical evidence – that requires discussion, question and answer, and learning to think in a way developed by historians.

Worthwhile Activities

We now come to a crucial point in the definition of education – the problem of worthwhile activities. Richard Peters' first principle was that education implied the transmission of what is worthwhile. But how do we decide what is worthwhile? What additional criteria must be involved here? At this stage, two warnings are necessary: first, that this is an extremely difficult area; and second, that no completely satisfactory answer has, in my view, yet been provided.

Nevertheless, there are issues of direct relevance to the teacher here and it is important for teachers to become aware of the arguments and issues involved, even if completely clear-cut solutions cannot be provided.

The first criterion of worthwhileness, according to Peters, is that the activity must be capable of going on for some time; activities which are too easily mastered will be less worthwhile than those which are more open-ended. The second criterion put forward by Peters is that of 'mutual compatibility'. This seems to be linked with the idea of balance; one worth while activity should not rule out others. A worthwhile activity should also not be in conflict with other aesthetic and moral principles – for example, the Marquis de Sade's torturing might fit in with the first criterion of open-endedness (it might be possible to go on inventing new tortures and deriving satisfaction from them), but torture would not be a worth while activity because it offends against the second criterion by being in conflict with other important moral principles such as respect for persons, not causing unnecessary pain, and so on. Another aspect of mutual compatibility is that a worth while activity should not be competitive – sporting prowess, making money, or collecting valuables are essentially competitive in the sense that if one person wins, no one else can. This is in contrast with knowledge about art and music, for example, mastery of which does not exclude access to the knowledge by others.

The application of these criteria results in such activities as science and philosophy being classified as worth while. They can be pursued without preventing others from pursuing them, and they are open-ended. 'Truth' is not an object which can be attained, nor is the abstract quality of beauty. An additional criterion is that worth while activities should be serious rather than trivial – thus games are excluded since they do not contribute to real life in any meaningful way. Playing cricket may be highly enjoyable or interesting, but it does not tell us anything about life outside the world of cricket. Science does – it explains certain aspects of the universe; so does literature. This set of criteria can be developed into a formula which seems to come up with more or less the right answers. The kinds of subjects which fit in with these criteria of worthwhileness are probably those which most rational people would want in a modern curriculum. But I do not find the explanations totally convincing. There are difficulties in this view of worthwhileness. On the first criterion – that the activity must be capable of going on for some time – there is no good reason, it seems to me, why this has to be built-in as a criterion. It may even be that this is an argument particularly appropriate for a society dominated by a leisured class for whom 'spending time' is a problem. Criteria 2 and 3 are also difficult in that they involve other principles: aesthetic and moral principles in the case of 2 — difficulties of definition of the 'serious' in criterion 3. I personally am sure science is more worthwhile than playing bingo, but I have doubts about the comparative worthwhileness of ballet and soccer. Are all games to be classified as trivial? Could we not say that chess, although a game, is more like mathematics than bingo? If we apply these criteria, does not music become a closed system (like a trivial game) and, therefore, inferior to literature (which gives us insights into the world of reality)?

It may be very difficult indeed to think of criteria of worthwhileness in the abstract. To some extent, it will be true that each society will develop its notions of worthwhileness. It will be an interesting problem for philosophy to see which aspects of worthwhileness must be universal, but I am not yet convinced that we have the correct formula for deciding even that.

An alternative approach is not to attempt to establish all the universal criteria, but to be satisfied with the task of deciding what could reasonably be regarded as worthwhile in our society today. Such an approach would involve a quite different line of argument. In England and Wales, education is compulsory from five until sixteen. Children are compelled to attend school and their parents are compelled to send their children to school. In return for this loss of liberty, the state has a duty to specify the supposed advantages of compulsory schooling. In order to do this, certain assumptions have to be made about valuable or worthwhile experiences in school. It has often been suggested that in a democratic society the state should endeavour to provide educational experiences that a good parent would want to provide for his own children. A good parent in this context would be one who is knowledgeable about education, is completely rational, and wants to prepare his child adequately for adult life in our society as well as to ensure he undergoes those educational experiences suitable for an enriched childhood. The ideal state system would provide for all children what the ideal parent provides for his own children, just as a parent with a sick child would want to give that child the treatment that a doctor would give his own children.[6]

This is simply another way of saying that the state should act positively in equalising opportunities for all children as far as this is possible. Two points need to be made in this respect: first, this equalisation will never be perfect in any society, but that should not prevent us from regarding the principle as a good one. (We have been much more ready to accept the idea of equality before the law than equality of opportunity in education. Most people realise that equality before the law is an ideal rather than reality – the rich can afford to hire better lawyers, take greater legal risks, and so on – but that does not mean that the ideal of equality before the law is not an excellent one.) The second point is that future generations (or perhaps even some theorists today) may not agree that what the state would provide (acting in the role of ideal parent) would, in practice, be the best for all children. It might eventually be discovered, for example, that teaching children mathematics at age seven is harmful to them (just as removing tonsils has fallen out of favour with medical experts, whereas a generation ago, the ideal parent would have followed the ideal medical practitioners' advice in this respect). The important criterion to be established is that the state should attempt to provide the best available education for all children given the present state of knowledge, or educational expertise.

This might now make our task somewhat easier. We simply have to ask, what would the ideal parent today want for his children in school? What would the ideal parent regard as those worthwhile activities so important that schools should transmit them? This kind of theoretical approach has the great advantage of being much closer to what good headteachers are already trying to do. The only difference would be that most teachers and headteachers would perhaps be working too closely within a traditional framework. Teaching is a very conservative profession, and most teachers tend to transmit what they were taught in the way they were instructed. What then would the ideal teacher want to regard as a comprehensive set of worthwhile activities, acting in his role of ideal parent substitute?

Before attempting to answer that question, since we have changed the basis of the argument from philosophy to sociology, it would be useful to insert a note about the sociology of education. Every society has the task of transmitting knowledge, skills and values to the young. Simple, pre-industrial societies have two advantages in this respect: first, change is usually much less rapid, so tradition can be followed with confidence – there is no need to rethink what needs to be taught, or how it should be taught; second, there is less social differentiation, less division of labour, so all young people learn more or less the same things. This being so, education can be carried out on an almost completely informal basis: girls will learn most of what they need to know by watching their mothers, older sisters and aunts; boys will learn from older male relatives and other members of the community. No formal schooling is necessary: boys need to become like their fathers, girls follow in their mothers' footsteps. The way of life is uncontroversial and unquestioned.

Modern societies are different in a number of ways. Life and knowledge are changing very rapidly – parents' knowledge is obsolete as their children are growing up. The division of labour is so complex that children do not necessarily follow the same careers as parents. Knowledge is specialised — some individuals need more knowledge than others. The invention of writing, and even more importantly printing, has made it necessary not only for the young to learn to read, but to understand a wide range of subject matter.

The third point in the preceding paragraph conceals an enormous problem. The fact that knowledge has become specialised, combined with the fact that different kinds of knowledge (and different levels of knowledge) are needed for different jobs, means that schools tend to get involved in the process of *selection* as well as in their rightful task of knowledge transmission. Because modern society demands that some will be skilled workers and others less skilled, schools have become places where the young are classified as successes and failures. This may appear irrelevant to the argument about what is worthwhile, but it is such a dominant feature of the schools that it cannot be ignored in this context. A 'good' parent will not only want a child to be given worthwhile knowledge, but will also want that child to be provided with a good 'job-ticket'.

In this respect, the state (or the headteacher) should make a careful distinction between these two kinds of desires. In a democratic society, schools should provide the worthwhile knowledge desired by the ideal parent, but not be concerned with the desired job-ticket (and not be concerned with all the selection processes involved with that).

We can now return to the question of what the ideal parent would consider to be worthwhile knowledge in our society today, but bearing in mind (so far as it is possible) the changes that are taking place and are likely to take place in society. I suggest that the ideal parents (ignoring job-tickets) would want:

(a) certain kinds of experience which would enrich their child's life and contribute to the enjoyment of life;
(b) certain kinds of knowledge which would help their child to understand the world and to participate effectively within it;
(c) the knowledge, attitudes and values which enable their child to develop into a 'good' member of society.

Each of these three categories of worthwhile activities needs further explanation.

Category (a) will include art, music, literature, and physical education (remaining for the moment with traditional subjects) as well as many other kinds of experience.

Category (b) would be especially concerned with science and technology, to give understanding of the physical environment; and with social sciences including history, geography and religious studies, to contribute an understanding of the social environment.

Category (c) would be concerned with social and moral education.

There is, of course, a good deal of overlap between these three major areas. English is required in all areas; mathematics in both (b) and (c), but might for many contribute enjoyment and satisfaction as well. The social sciences are located mainly in (b), but will be of considerable relevance in (c), and so on.

The worth while is, therefore, defined in terms of the knowledge and experience which help to relate children to their society. This assumes that the distinction often made by naive educational progressives, that there is a necessary opposition between the needs of the child and the needs of society, is completely false. Once the job-ticket aspect of schooling is removed, it is possible to say that education is concerned with enabling the young to understand their environment and to enjoy it; becoming part of society does not involve a loss of identity quite the opposite, as an individual only becomes truly human by understanding the relationship between the individual and the social.[7]

This formula will, of course, only work for our own society and others like it. Sparta and Rome would have had different values and different views of the worth while. The key characteristics of Western society are that we are a highly industrialised society, placing a high value on science and technology, and also that we are a democratic society with a commitment to social justice. What we regard as worthwhile is, therefore, partly a question of technology and the resulting social structure and partly a question of values, some of which may be 'universal' rather then 'local'.

Summary

Education is different from schooling and from instruction. In a democratic society education must be available for all. We return to the problem of deciding what kind of education is appropriate for all. Since it is so difficult to arrive at a philosophically accepted 'formula' for deciding what is 'worthwhile', then a pragmatic approach might be adopted: that is, giving to all children what an ideal parent would choose for his own children. The complicating factor is that, in our society, education is closely related to job-selection. This factor has to be disentangled from purely educational criteria.

NOTES

1 **The word 'metaphysical'** is used almost as a term of abuse by some philosophers. Recently, however, there have been attempts to reinstate metaphysics in mainstream philosophy. Metaphysics can be an attempt to characterise reality as a whole instead of being subdivided into particular aspects of existence. R.G. Collingwood in his

Essay on Metaphysics (1940) saw metaphysics as the interpretation of the 'absolute presuppositions' underlying the characteristic thought of any particular period of history.

2 **Traditional sociology of education** tended to concentrate on such topics as social class differences in educational achievement. The new sociologists of education in the 1960s and 1970s criticised this approach for 'taking' problems rather than 'making' them. They felt that sociologists should question all aspects of education, including the content of the curriculum, rather than take them for granted. This has enlivened sociological debate considerably, but has often involved sociologists in long-standing philosophical problems about which they argue at a naive level. *See Class, Culture and the Curriculum* Lawton (1975), Chapter 4.

3 **At this point** you may ask, 'But who says what is morally objectionable?' The attempt to avoid the metaphysics is not the same as avoiding value judgments. It will be up to the philosophers who make judgments about what is and what is not morally objectionable, to justify their position in rational terms. Education cannot be value-free, but values should be made explicit and should be justified in rational terms.

4 **The hidden curriculum, the paracurriculum.** Clearly, not everything that is learned in school is contained in the official curriculum or set of syllabuses. It has often been pointed out, for example, that certain values are intentionally transmitted by means of such extra-curricular activities as community service, or by aspects of the school organisation such as the prefect system. The term 'hidden curriculum' has been used to cover such kinds of learning, but since some of these activities are by no means hidden, David Hargreaves has suggested the term 'paracurriculum'. According to R.S. Peters, education must be 'carried out with the full awareness of what is being learned by both pupils and teachers'. In terms of the 'paracurriculum' an interesting point, therefore, emerges. Can anything be learnt by means of the prefect system, for example, which can be said to be truly educational?

5 **It would be difficult** to argue against those who might suggest that there is too much instruction and too little education in many of our schools. On the other hand, it would be a strange school that abolished instruction altogether.

6 **This approach** to establishing a worthwhile curriculum is closely related to the principles of social justice put forward by John Rawls (to be discussed in Chapter 6). If we have a clear idea about what a worthwhile curriculum would be, then it should be available for all pupils, not a privileged minority. If we are not absolutely sure about what should be included in a worthwhile curriculum, we must act on the best advice obtainable, and then make that programme available for all pupils.

7 **See Chapters 6 and 8** for an elaboration of the argument about the false dichotomy between the individual and society. It is one of the basic assumptions of this book that there is no necessary conflict between the needs of the individual and what is good for society. Human beings only become truly human by social interaction. That is not to say that there are no social influences which ought not to be resisted in education.

6 Social and Philosophical Issues in Education

Chapter 5 ended with an assertion that there was no contradiction between the needs of the individual and the needs of society. That is not to say that there is no such conflict, only that there need not be one. That point now has to be argued out in greater detail. We will then proceed to related topics of equality in education, the common school, and religious and moral education.

The idea that there is a conflict between the needs of the individual and the needs of society goes back to Rousseau. Rousseau saw society as an evil, corrupting influence. It should be borne in mind, however, that this was in the context of eighteenth-century France, with a harsh despotic government. Rousseau was fond of contrasting the civilised society that he knew with life in simple pre-industrial societes. We should perhaps also remember that Rousseau was writing at the time that stories of exotic pre-industralised societies were filtering back into Europe from Tahiti and other apparently idyllic, uncivilised societies.

A similar point of view has been adopted by some Marxists, who suggest that man is good, but society – meaning capitalist society – tends to corrupt. Yet Marxists do not deny the importance of the social; even if society is less than perfect, man has to learn to live within it as there is no alternative. An additional point I would make is that whether we want to change society or conserve it exactly as it is, an individual still needs to understand it. So every individual needs to be inducted into language, history, literature, science, and social science.

Given this role of mediating between the individual and society, the school becomes a most important influence, and much will depend on its quality as an institution.

At least four changes would be necessary in most schools. The first is that the school should face up to the conflict between genuine educational needs and the provision of job-tickets – that is, servicing the labour market.[1] Schools will not be able to do this without considerable support from the central authority in education. Secondly, schools need to humanise teacher/pupil relationships. Too many schools tend to be anonymous, with unreasonable rules. The shadow of nineteenth-century workhouses still hangs over far too many schools. Thirdly, schools should be places which are good for teachers as well as pupils. Some schools today are good for neither. Much needs to be done to make teachers share in making decisions. Finally, schools should be places where hard work takes place without a feeling of oppression. Much of the detailed comments I have made about teaching and learning should be applied in this context.

One major change in education since the nineteenth century has been the establishment of a much more humane attitude to children in schools, although this ideal has still to be translated into practice in some schools, and made less extreme and more workable in other schools claiming to be progressive. This process can be seen as part of an 'emancipation' movement: slaves were freed in the nineteenth century, women emancipated and children regarded as individuals with rights in the twentieth century.

A similar trend can be seen in the movement towards social justice and equality of opportunity in education. It has gradually been accepted that rich and poor should be equal before the law, that working people shoule be able to vote and participate in the running of the country, and that certain aspects of life should be regarded as a right (for example, good housing and health care). Furthermore, since 1944 it has been official policy to foster equality of opportunity in education.

Equality in Education

In the nineteenth century it was taken for granted that the children of the rich and the children of the poor should have totally different kinds of educational experiences. The question then was not whether there should be equality of opportunity, but whether there should be any education at all for the poor. When after 1833 the state became involved, the education provided in what later were called elementary schools, was deliberately inferior to what middle-class and upper-class parents were paying for. This tradition continued throughout the nineteenth century with many modifications, and into the twentieth century. But by the beginning of the twentieth century, elementary education was established and a demand began to be made for access to secondary education for working-class children. 'Secondary education for all' became a slogan for the Trades Union Congress and the newly-formed Labour Party.[2] Only in 1944, however, was this achieved — free, compulsory education for *all* from age five to age fourteen, later fifteen and eventually sixteen.

But was this the same as equality of opportunity in education? As we saw in Chapters 1 and 3, several problems remained in this respect: one was that the kind of education made available after 1944 to eleven-year-old pupils was extremely varied in quality from one school to another; another was that the method of selection was dubious.[3] On a national basis it could never have been claimed that the most suitable children were actually being selected as the 20% or so grammar pupils. A much more fundamental question was eventually asked about the appropriateness in a democracy of merely replacing social elitism by intellectual elitism. Why should it be regarded as more just to give a child a superior education because he had a high IQ than because his father had a high income? What was meant by equality and by equality of opportunity in education?[4]

Opponents of the ideal of equality in educational opportunity often make fun of the egalitarian viewpoint[5] by suggesting that it is obvious to everyone that children are not equal. This is deliberately to confuse the issue. The essential point being made by egalitarians is that all children at, say, the age of eleven (or any other age) should have equality of access to worthwhile educational experiences irrespective of sex, religion, race, or social background. This is manifestly not the case in England: at one extreme we have independent schools for those who can afford the very high fees, and have the necessary social connections to gain access; next we have other independent schools of slightly lower social status, but still requiring the payment of high fees; within the state system after 1944 it was soon shown that even with free secondary education, middle-class children tended to have a better chance of gaining access to grammar schools, and working-class children were consigned to secondary modern schools which were little different in many cases from the old elementary schools. Many complained that the

1944 Act had achieved very little for certain categories of children.[6]

The result was a gradual move to comprehensive secondary education (leaving the question of independent schools unsolved). Finally, with the widespread establishment of comprehensive schools, attention was paid to fairer methods of organisation within those schools, such as the replacement of streaming by a more flexible structure such as setting, and, finally, the question of the curriculum was tackled. It was suggested that the common school had the task of transmitting to all pupils a common culture by means of a common curriculum. These ideas, especially those of the common school and the common curriculum, are now being seriously challenged. The Conservative Government in 1979-80 introduced legislation for an 'assisted places scheme' which would remove 'bright' pupils from comprehensive schools and send them to fee-paying independent schools.

There are two main anti-egalitarian arguments in the field of education. The first states that to treat unequals equally is potentially as unfair and harmful as treating equals unequally. This argument has a good pedigree, being derived from Aristotle, but is capable of several different interpretations. At first sight, it would seem to be quite reasonable to say that if you have two children, one blind and the other sighted, it would be wrong to treat them equally – the blind child needs many extra facilities. So far, so good! But the same argument can be used to justify treating unequally a child who is more intelligent than another child, by giving the intelligent child *more* educational facilities (because he will benefit more from them). I have even heard the argument used that it would be unjust to treat a rich child on equal terms with a poor child because the rich child's parents have given him higher expectations!

The other argument against equality, or rather in favour of unequal treatment, is on grounds of liberty. This argument has a number of variations, but basically it amounts to the following: 'Social justice is a good thing, but so is liberty. If they are ever in conflict, liberty must be regarded as more important, because life in an unfree society would be intolerable.' Translated into educational terms this would mean that, for example, people should be free to spend their money in whatever way they wish – some will spend money on drink or gambling, or buying a new car, so it would be intolerable if parents were prevented from spending their money on their children's education...

It would be possible to criticise this point of view with a number of arguments, such as that it is a strange notion of liberty which applies it only to the rich, or that it is by no means self-evident that liberty is in its total form more important than social justice in any society. But at this stage I should like to put forward the views of Rawls on social justice, and then try to apply them to the specific case of education.

Rawls' Theory of Justice

John Rawls is an American philosopher whose book *A Theory of Justice* (1972) has been enormously influential in philosophical circles, but has not, as far as I know, been applied directly to educational issues in this country. Rawls puts forward his argument about justice in the form of a fable or hypothetical society. Suppose a group of people was required to draw up rules for a fair society. Perhaps the most effective way would be for them to draw up these rules not knowing what position they would eventually occupy in the society once it came into existence.[7] It may be useful to invite the reader to join in this game: try to draw up a set of rules that would be fair for a new society. Make sure they are really fair, because when you join that society, you may be either a man or woman, Black or White, Catholic or Protestant, rich or poor, intelligent or not so intelligent, and so on ... What principles would you establish?

Rawls suggests that given that situation the only possible set of rules which could emerge would be a code of practice which always gave the benefit of the doubt, or a possible advantage, to the underdog, to the less privileged.[8] The fact that most societies seem to work in the opposite direction (that is, giving more to those who are already privileged) is perhaps an indication of the social position of those in positions of power and with the duty of making decisions.

It would follow from this premiss that people should be treated equaly unless there are good reasons for doing otherwise, and that where there are good reasons, the advantage should always go to the less privileged. This is not in conflict with the Aristotelian view that it would be unfair to treat unequals equally, it merely provides a rule for deciding how they should be treated once we have decided that it would not be fair to treat them equally. It would, of course, rule out one of the examples given above, namely giving a better education to a rich child because of his higher expectations.

If we now apply these principles to education, the results would be quite dramatic. Since the money to be spent on education is limited, the same amount should be spent on all pupils (or perhaps all pupils of the same age) unless good reason can be shown otherwise. If a case is made for differential spending, more should be spent on the handicapped compared with the normal, more should be spent on children with lower than average intelligence than on those with above average intelligence; more should be spent on working class than on middle class children; more should be spent on Black children than on White children; more should be spent on girls than on boys . . . and so on. In fact, with most of those examples the opposite is the case in our society.

There would be many obvious difficulties in applying these principles in practice, but that should not blind us to the fact that the principle itself seems extremely reasonable. It would also be very uncomfortable for privileged individuals in society if it was accepted. Public schools would have to be transformed immediately into institutions for the less privileged. Eton and Harrow might be ideal educational environments for the children of deprived parents, one-parent families, immigrant children and others with extreme learning difficulties!

Can the Rawls principle also be applied to the organisation of state schools generally? It would seem to favour comprehensive schools rather than separate grammar schools for the more intelligent (unless, of course, those schools were given less well qualified teachers and less money to spend on books and equipment). It would also seem to favour a common curriculum within the common school (unless good reason could be shown otherwise). But a *caveat* needs to be inserted at this point: 'treated equally' does not mean 'treated exactly the same'. There would be enormous difficulties in interpreting that qualification, but it would foolish from an educational point of view to try to treat children as though they were all the same in their needs. It would also be foolish to expect equality of outcome as well as equality of opportunity. Neither a common curriculum nor equality of opportunity implies that all children will end up the same, or indeed that they should have exactly the same kind of curriculum. What is clear is that the principle would not permit, for example, some children to study physics and chemistry while others were given a walk around the gas works instead of science. Only if the gas works curriculum represented a genuinely effective method of teaching science to those who found it difficult to understand scientific ideas without direct experience, would it be a perfectly legitimate route to worthwhile knowledge. Educationists would, however, always have to be extremely vigilant that the 'rules' were being interpreted consistently in favour of the less privileged. It would be all too easy to represent an inferior curriculum as simply an alternative route.

In the cause of equality, therefore, schools should be encouraged to develop alternative effective methods, and also to expect different levels of achievement within the worthwhile areas. A common curriculum is not a uniform curriculum; equality of opportunity is not treating everyone the same, still less expecting identical achievement. But differential treatment must be justifiable in terms of giving more or better to the less fortunate.

Continuing Education

The idea of equality of educational opportunity if implemented along the lines suggested above, would be almost revolutionary in that it runs counter to so many established views and traditions in English education. There are signs, however, that such a change is necessary, because the existing pattern of 'end on' education is inefficient and out of date as well as unjust. Especially since the end of the Second World War in 1945 a number of suggestions have been made for *education permanente,* recurrent education, lifelong education, or continuing education. These terms have slightly different shades of meaning, but all involve the idea that a society's educational planning should not be concerned with a period of schooling, or of schooling plus Further or Higher Education (the 'end on' pattern referred to above), but should be thought of in terms of an individual's whole life span. There is a strong egalitarian flavour to much of the writing in this field, but no question of uniformity is envisaged. A wide variety of educational routes is one of the features of recurrent or continuing education.

There is among the advocates of continuing education general agreement that there should be a period of compulsory schooling to begin with, ending at fifteen or possibly later. Most countries now seem to be moving to a pattern of a primary-secondary break at about the age of eleven or twelve, followed by a common secondary educational experience which is retained for as long as possible before dividing into various vocational, Further or Higher educational paths.

At age sixteen, say, some will stay at school, some will go on to vocational education in a college of Further Education or its equivalent, some will go to work and continue education on a part-time basis. But as a principle some educational provision should be compulsory up to about the age of eighteen or nineteen. The UK is lagging behind in this respect very badly.

Some eighteen or nineteen-year-olds still at school may decide to proceed directly to university, but that is not necessarily the most appropriate route in the eyes of advocates of continuing education. A certain amount of work experience in between school and university might be advantageous, it is suggested, even for those who are committed to an academic career. Other young people going on to a university degree would take some kind of sandwich course (that is, a mixture of theory and practical work experience). Continuing education would involve an expansion of that kind of work in universities (or in the case of the UK in polytechnics). Others people would (in the UK) work part-time for technical qualifications such as those offered by TEC (Technician Education Council) and BEC (Business Education Council) which would lead to further qualifications.

Another major innovation would be that all workers, not just the highly qualified, would be considered to need and to deserve periods of full-time study at intervals throughout their working life. Paid educational leave should be provided for this purpose (many trade unions in the UK are now incorporating this factor into their negotiations with employers; paid educational leave is already a legal requirement in many continental countries). These periods of full-time study could be either to bring technical qualifications up to date (a major idea behind recurrent education), or to develop social and political skills (trade union studies), or to enrich leisure in a variety of ways.

In addition, a planned programme of continuing education would include much greater emphasis on what has been conventionally referred to as adult education (which does not include vocational studies). This would again be of three main kinds: technical, socio-political and recreational, with one important extra dimension – 'remedial'. 'Remedial' in this context would cover a wide range of possiblities, but all would involve making good the deficiencies or failures of the school system. Provision would range from special classes for illiterates to basic education in mathematics and science and other areas of the common curriculum. The purpose would be two-fold: to put right earlier failures, and to provide a continuing link with further, more advanced, studies.

This may sound idealistic, and unfortunately many aspects of this programme, which already exist in embryo, tend to be hardest hit by cuts in public expenditure. But a good deal of progress has been made in Europe (see especially publications of the European Economic Community and the Council of Europe),[9] and many educationists see continuing education not only as an area most likely to develop in the next ten or twenty years, but also as an important ideal which could serve to reform the whole of an educational system. It is important also because it encourages the idea of education as a set of rights of access rather than something to be enforced on the reluctant young. Continuing education is, therefore, not to be confused with the idea of a more extensive system of adult education. It is an ideal which would encourage us to think in terms of education from the cradle to the grave.

Religious and Moral Education

If education is compulsory, is it right that religious education and moral education should be part of the school curriculum? This is perhaps a particularly pertinent question today, since our society is now much less a religious society than during the mid-nineteenth century when it was taken for granted that religious education should be one of the basic subjects in elementary schools and in secondary and public schools. An additional problem today is the fact that we are a multi-cultural society, and many of the minority cultures have religions other than Christianity. A further question is the extent to which moral education can be taught within religious education or should be regarded as entirely separate from it.

When the clauses dealing with religious education in the 1944 Education Act were discussed in the House of Commons, there was little debate about them.[10] The clauses were accepted with very little controversy aroused. Perhaps this was because, at that time, not much thought was given to the principles of moral education, and it was assumed that religious instruction was the only means of passing on the basic ethical values of our society to the next generation. Today, it is generally agreed by Christians and non-Christians alike that the present arrangements for religious education in most schools are unsatisfactory as a means of teaching about religion and Christianity. They are even less satisfactory as a means of teaching moral education. Religious instruction as a means of moral education might be satisfactory in a society where there was a commitment to one religion, but for a society which is largely secular to rely on the teaching of religious doctrines as a basis for moral behaviour is dangerous and illogical. There is a great need for elementary ethics to be introduced to young people in some way, and there is no reason to think that this would be any more difficult than the introduction of other value issues. There are also good arguments for suggesting that religious education in a multi-cultural society should be religious studies rather than trying to inculcate particular doctrines of a single religion or denomination. The exception to this might be in denominational schools where religious instruction would consist of passing on a particular set of beliefs or doctrines, although this is increasingly questioned as a desirable part of the curriculum by a number of religious bodies themselves.

The greatest need is for young people to be helped to develop a rational basis for moral behaviour. Schools have a part to play in this, but they should not under-estimate the difficulties involved. Too many headteachers claim that they are indulging in moral education 'all the time', but find it less easy to specify when or how. Probably, the most important point to be made by teachers is that values and morals are *not* simply a matter of taste, and it is not necessary to believe in heaven and hell to see that one form of behaviour is better than another. This point can be made by teachers of subjects other than religious education, perhaps more effectively; as long as they know what they are doing, specialists in, say, English literature, or history, have many opportunities to discuss questions of right and wrong behaviour as a natural part of their own subject matter. For example, was not the quality of moral life better (not just different) in Athens than in Sparta? Were not the Nazi atrocities in the Second World War immoral by any acceptable code of morality? Teachers have a great responsibility to examine concepts such as relativism, its usefulness as well as its limitations. We should all be relativists in the sense of having respect for other cultures, and not taking it for granted that our own ways are always best; but it is equally important to show that any set of rules is not necessarily as good as any other, and that we could not survive as a society with no rules at all. Popper (1966) has made the useful point that to say that social rules or moral norms or aesthetic criteria are man-made does *not* necessarily lead us to the conclusion that they are arbitrary. It might be interesting to begin with some rules which seem to be irrational or arbitrary (for example, British licensing laws), and then to contrast them with rules which are necessary and completely justifiable (for example, laws against rape or murder).

Two points need to be made in conclusion. The first is that there is now very good evidence to suggest that children in order to reach moral autonomy need to be taught moral concepts (and we can settle for nothing less than moral autonomy in a democratic secular society); and that they also should be given practice in moral discussions and decision-making. Second, if teachers are going to undertake this task they also need special training in both the content of moral education and the appropriate teaching methods.[11]

Finally, a distinction needs to be made between religious instruction and religious studies or religious education. 'Religious instruction' would seem to indicate the inculcation of religious doctrines of a denominational kind (although this is contrary to Clause 26 of the Education Act of 1944). That would now seem to be out of place, except in denominational schools. But there are much stronger arguments for teaching young people about comparative religion as well as their own cultural heritage. This more neutral approach would also be much more appropriate in a multi-cultural, pluralistic society.

Summary

In this chapter we return to the problem of the individual and society — Rousseau's idea that there was a conflict between the individual child's educational needs and the demands of a potentially corrupting society. It is suggested that the problem is much more complex than 'freedom versus conformity' because individuals only become fully human by interaction with others and by being inducted into significant aspects of the common culture. The views of John Rawls on justice are applied to educational provision: in order to achieve some educational goals, lifelong education rather than just 'schooling' will be necessary. Finally, the importance of moral understanding is emphasised as an essential aspect of education in modern, secular society.

NOTES

1 **Recently** there has been an unfortunate tendency to emphasise this aspect of schooling (i.e., providing employers with the kind of labour that they say they need). Employers have complained about the quality of young workers joining their offices and factories, and in particular, have criticised schools for not achieving high standards in English and arithmetic. These complaints should not be ignored, but it must always be emphasised that job training is not the major function of education. It is the function of schools to prepare the young for adult life, including work, but it is not the function of the schools to indulge in specific vocational training. This is not to say, nevertheless, that there is no justification for some of the complaints being made about poor standards.

2 **The importance of the Labour Party** in the campaign for secondary education for all is a controversial issue. Parkinson (1970) suggests that Labour Party policy was an attempt to implement socialist ideals of equality and the right to self-development; Barker (1972) argues that the Labour Party has rarely pursued socialist policies in education, and has usually carried on with Liberal or even Tory Party policies whenever it was in office. *See also* Lawton (1977) who suggests that there have always been two groups within the Labour Party — an elitist group more in favour of grammar schools and selection, and an egalitarian group in favour of comprehensive schools and equality of opportunity.

3 *See* Chapter 1, Note 9 (p. 23), on Brian Simon's work in this field. Also *see* Olive Banks (1955).

4 *See* Note 2 above. Many educational reformers in the early part of the twentieth century saw the problem of social justice as one of giving bright working-class children the opportunity which less bright middle-class children already possessed because their parents could pay school fees. This was one motive behind abolishing fees for secondary education. Giving poorer children scholarships in the 1920s and 1930s

was also an expression of this point of view. It was extremely useful at that time, but it represents a very limited view of fairness in educational opportunity. Perhaps the confusion has arisen because in the years following 1944 there was very little agreement about what secondary education should consist of. Without a view of what constituted a suitable secondary education for all, it was perhaps inevitable that the only kind of education which was regarded as worthwhile was the traditional very academic one. If we really believe in social justice, however, we have to find a form of secondary education which is suitable for all pupils. This is not to say that there will not be differences within secondary education, merely that all pupils must have a right to something which is worthy of their time.

5 **The naive objection** to the egalitarian viewpoint is that it is simply not true that all men or all children are equal — some children are tall, some are short; some can run faster than others. Of course, children are very different from one another; the point is, should they be treated differently in education because of irrelevant factors?

6 **Julienne Ford** (1969). Ford discovered, in a study of a limited number of comprehensive schools, that in those schools where rigid forms of streaming were practised, the working-class children were still very much at a disadvantage compared with middle-class children. Working-class children tended to under-achieve and to be over-represented in the lower streams. This has given rise to suggestions about more flexible arrangements for segregating children such as setting.

7 **Rawls** refers to this procedure as the 'veil of ignorance' technique. Because we are all not completely devoid of selfishness, we could only guarantee disinterested decisions if we assume that the decision-maker had no axe to grind, and most importantly, no beliefs about social priorities.

8 **This is, in fact, Rawls's second principle.** The first principle is that it would be agreed that everyone should have the basic liberties (to vote, to speak on political matters, etc.) — that is, no one would wish to take the risk of not being free in a society any more than they would want to risk being an underdog in a society which was unfair (the second principle). Rawls also puts forward the principle of priority whereby the first principle takes precedence over the second — that is, we only begin to discuss fairness when the basic liberties have been satisfied.

9 **For example,** the Council of Europe publication *Organisation, Content and Methods of Adult Education* (1977). (Council of Europe publications are distributed in the UK by Her Majesty's Stationery Office.)

10 **In the 1944 Education Act** religious instruction is the only compulsory subject (but parents have the right to withdraw children from those lessons).

11 **Interesting materials on moral education** have been produced by the Schools Council Moral Education Project directed by Peter McPhail. P.R. May carried out a survey in 1967 on the attitudes of teachers to moral and religious education. Over 60% agreed that special periods should be set aside for moral education. May suggests some ways in which this work could be undertaken. Courses could be mounted in elementary psychology concerning the way individuals develop intellectually, emotionally and morally, and how attitudes are formed and changed. Pupils should also be trained in educating the emotions, etc. *See* May (1971).

7 Curriculum Planning

Curriculum planning cannot be value free, and it cannot take place in an ideological vacuum. Planning is simply a means of translating values and purposes into reality. [1] It is important to realise that a planning model may be far from neutral, and may influence and even distort the intentions of the educationists involved. It is, therefore, very important that theorists should not be satisfied with outlining a set of programme ideals, but should be prepared to get involved in their implementation.

Planning must begin with first principles. Whatever else education is concerned with, it is certainly concerned with the transmission of knowledge and ideas from one generation to the next. Educationists are, therefore, inevitably involved in questions such as, 'What is knowledge?', or 'How is knowledge classified or sub-divided?' If we are to plan the transmission of knowledge, we must have some kind of theory or model to use as a basis of planning. But first it is necessary to be clear about the kind of knowledge values or dispositions that we wish to transmit. [2] In Chapter 5, a good deal of time was spent on discussing worthwhile knowledge, but there are also fundamental questions about the nature of knowledge which are extremely relevant to teachers. Primary and secondary school teachers tend to see these questions differently. Primary school teachers tend to see knowledge as a 'seamless garment' and see their role as being concerned with knowledge as a whole, whereas secondary school teachers, having spent several years becoming 'specialists', tend to see knowledge neatly sub-divided into subjects or disciplines.

Another important contrast is that philosophers and sociologists approach knowledge very differently. Philosophers tend to look for the logical characteristics of different kinds of knowledge or forms of knowledge; sociologists tend to see knowledge arising out of the social structure or division of labour.[3]

In a simple society, knowledge will tend to be seen as a unity: there will be no difference between religious and political knowledge, or 'scientific' and poetic knowledge. Knowledge is knowledge, and important knowledge will be transmitted to the next generation. There may be specialists in certain kinds of knowledge — for example, someone who is an expert in knowledge about spells, sorcery, or magic, or a tribal elder whose memory of folk-lore and legend is extensive — but knowledge is not divided neatly into compartments. Dividing knowledge into subjects was partly the result of the idea of division of labour and partly the outcome of philosophical analysis. By the time of the classical Greek civilisation, philosophers were able to talk of 'subjects' such as mathematics and poetry: Plato felt that mathematics was infinitely superior to other forms of knowledge. Similarly, the Greeks after Aristotle made an important distinction between physics and metaphysics.

By the middle ages, sufficient distinctions were made to divide the curriculum into two stages — the trivium and the more advanced quadrivium.[4] The age of academic specialisation was already with us: the peasant would make no sense of such distinctions, but university teachers and students would begin to take them for granted.

The educated man of the Renaissance was still expected to be acquainted with all the available disciplines, but by the nineteenth century it was impossible for any individual to be completely conversant with knowledge as it then existed. In 1959, C. P. Snow[5] pointed out the great disadvantage of an education system which divided people into two camps: 'science' or 'arts'.

Later in this chapter we will need to look into the question of the philosophical justification for such divisions of knowledge into subject compartments. But before we reach that it may be an advantage to look at the sociology of knowledge in a little more depth.

In the account I have just given of the development of divisions or subjects in the structure of knowledge, I have presented this as though it was necessarily linear development — that is, that the same kind of process happens naturally as societies develop in any part of the world. This may be misleading unless qualified. There are two basic ideas arising out of the sociology of knowledge. The first is that 'reality' is not everywhere perceived in the same way; the second is that within a given culture (and especially in more advanced complex societies) different members of society will have different kinds of access to knowledge, and different perceptions of reality which will tend to be related to their position in the social structure.

The first idea goes back at least as far as Pascal, who suggested that what is truth on one side of the Pyrenees may be error on the other side. The second idea may be graphically illustrated by an example which Donald MacRae quotes from W. P. Ker's *Epic and Romance:* 'the seigneur whose trade is war wants information about the strong city of Nimes: he is answered by a peasant with facts about how much bread costs there, and the problem of paying toll. It is not that the serf is stupid; he merely conceives the same world in largely different terms from his feudal superior, though on many matters of loyalty and religion he would share with the knight the latter's ideology' (MacRae 1961, p. 72).

Karl Mannheim[6] was much concerned with the sociology of knowledge, and the problem of the social disposition of knowledge in a society. Much of Mannheim's writing is concerned with the fact that different social strata in a society have only limited access to knowledge (or limited ways of perceiving reality). He felt that people at different levels in society perceived the world differently because they had acquired different kinds of skills occupationally and different kinds of knowledge. In this respect, he was close to the Marxist view that a person's consciousness is determined by his relationship to the means of production. Mannheim asserted that society determines not only the appearance but also the content of 'ideation' (except for mathematics and some kinds of science). Perceiving the world of reality is not like taking a photograph with a camera; we inevitably see reality through a kind of cultural lens which will distort reality to some extent. The way that artists paint reality, or poets describe reality, or even the way that historians write about the past is, according to Mannheim and others, a distorted view, coloured by their own particular position in society.

Mannheim's concern was particularly with 'ideology' which he used in a much narrower sense than some other sociologists to mean the false, or limited, view of reality held by the ruling class. The ruling class view of reality, or ideology, was necessarily distorted because it was incomplete; it also tended to be a conservative or reactionary view of reality, because the ruling class had a vested interest in preserving the world much as it was since almost any kind of social change might involve loss of privileges. Mannheim uses the word 'relationism' to denote the fact that, in his view, knowledge is always knowledge from a certain social position. Mannheim thought that ideologising influences could not be eradicated completely from an individual's or a group's perception of reality, but they could be modified by the systematic analysis of as many of the positions as possible. Mannheim also felt that different groups varied in their ability to transcend their own reality, and he believed that the group which was most favourably placed was the 'socially unattached intelligentsia'. This group was relatively free of class interest and many of the intelligentsia were 'marginal' or almost classless in the sense that they had moved out of one class without being committed to the reality system of another. Mannheim saw this kind of social mobility as very important to objectifying reality — it is also perhaps significant that he had himself undergone such a transition not only socially but also geographically (from a central European setting to the world of an English university).

There is a basic similarity between Marx and Mannheim in their stress on class, and the importance they give to the ruling class in the distribution of knowledge and the stratification of knowledge. They also agree that certain kinds of knowledge — science and mathematics — are less likely to be distorted than others such as history and literature.

More recent sociologists of knowledge have extended this argument to suggest that all knowledge is socially constructed and that subjects, for example, are simply the result of our particular class-based society.[7] By some the argument is even extended to suggest that knowledge and the rationality itself are merely conventions. But one of the difficulties with Marx, Mannheim, and later sociologists of knowledge, is that their argument that ideas are a product of social position can be applied to their own writing. For example, Bertrand Russell (1946) made the following observation:

> No man would engage in the pursuit of philosophy if he thought that *all* philosophy is *merely* an expression of irrational bias. But, every philosopher will agree that many other philosophers have been actuated by bias, and have had extra-rational reasons, of which they were usually unconscious, for many of their opinions. Marx, like the rest, believed in the truth of his own doctrines; he

> does not regard them as nothing but an expression of the feelings natural to a rebellious middle class German Jew in the middle of the nineteenth century. (p. 751)

This is a very important question. Why should Marx, Mannheim, and more recent sociologists of knowledge be exempt from their own view about the social determinism of knowledge? If rationality is simply a custom or a matter of taste, is there any point in sociologists talking to each other, let alone writing books?

This is not to say, of course, that there is no truth in what Marx, Mannheim and others stated, simply that we must be aware of exaggerated positions. It is now fairly well accepted by sociologists and philosophers alike that reality is not simply something 'out there'. Our perception is coloured by our own cultural experiences and our own upbringing. One of the problems for philosophers (and one of very great relevance to teachers) is to be able to disentangle what is 'true' in any meaningful sense from what is simply a matter of taste or custom.

One way of looking at history is to see it as the story of human beings interacting with their environment, interpreting the process of interaction in various ways, and acquiring some mastery and control over that environment. The accumulated experience of many generations can be called knowledge. Each generation has three tasks: learning the knowledge acquired by previous generations; adding to it and modifying the interpretation; and passing this revision on to the next generation. I suggested above that if a culture is simple, everything may be regarded as common sense, but when skills and technology become more complex, learning and knowledge become more specialised. No one person can master all the specialised branches of knowledge.

One aspect of human learning is developing the power to generalise: every incident in experience is unique, but we have to learn to see relationships between these unique experiences. For this we need concepts. Concepts are formed by grouping particular incidents or objects into classes: we conceptualise by classifying. But language development and conceptual development are concerned with more than single concepts or generalisations. We have to learn to link some concepts together and to exclude others in order to form 'conceptual systems'. Language development in particular is concerned with learning what words or groups of words fit together in one context but not in another. A group of conceptual systems may add up to what we refer to as a 'discipline'. Trying to decide whether the disciplines are man-made or God-given [8] is perhaps a fruitless exercise. What we have to decide is the extent to which working with disciplines is a useful way of proceeding in curricular planning, or whether it is a hindrance to learning or to certain kinds of learning. There is a strange dislike on the part of 'progressives' of subjects or disciplines, but the balance of evidence would seem to suggest (see also Chapter 3) that teaching and learning in terms of disciplines is an efficient way of structuring experience and knowledge. [9] This is not to say, of course, that all kinds of commonsense and everyday knowledge can be neatly fitted into one particular discipline or subject. The art of curriculum planning will be concerned with both using disciplines in so far as they are helpful to learning and combining disciplines and subjects where this would be more effective.

There are many approaches to the structure of knowledge and its application to curriculum planning. In America, J. J. Schwab [10] has been particularly influential. In England, the best known work on the structure and organisation of knowledge is that of Professor Paul Hirst. [11] Hirst suggests that all knowledge that man has achieved can be seen to be differentiated into a number of logically distinct forms. He contends that knowledge is possible only because of the use of patterns of related concepts in terms of which our experience is intelligible. Forms of knowledge can be distinguished from each other in three ways. First, within each form there are distinct types of concepts that characterise different types of knowledge; second, the concepts occur within different networks whose relationships determine what meaningful propositions can be made; and third, the forms of knowledge can be distinguished by different types of truth tests or validity tests.

According to Hirst, there are seven forms of knowledge:

1 mathematics and formal logic;
2 the physical sciences;
3 the human sciences including history;
4 moral understanding;
5 religion;
6 philosophy;
7 aesthetics.

Hirst put forward these ideas in a paper in 1965. In a later paper

'The Forms of Knowledge Revisited' (1974) he placed less emphasis on the idea of distinguishing forms of knowledge by the methodology employed for assessing true propositions. Hirst still believes that forms of knowledge are distinguishable in that way, but only in a secondary sense and he would not wish to emphasise that feature.

Hirst has, from time to time, been criticised for his forms of knowledge thesis, sometimes because he has not done enough work to justify some of the seven forms (why, for example, should there be a separate religious form? Is this not begging a number of questions about truth and validity?); sometimes because the seven, and the divisions between them, seem arbitrary (are not some aspects of the human sciences more like the physical sciences, for example?).

But in my view the value of this basic work remains. Hirst does not claim that it is a fully worked-out theory, but it would seem to be the best theory available at the moment. It is important for teachers and pupils to grasp that mathematics is a different kind of experience from history, and that science and literature are concerned with different kinds of 'truth'. It is also important for teachers to think more in terms of the network of concepts and processes which comprise a discipline, so that learning becomes less an accumulation of facts and more an understanding of a structure. For Hirst, learning a discipline is closely connected with learning the language of the discipline — language in this sense including the 'grammar' as well as the vocabulary.

It is also important to stress that Hirst sees a direct link between forms of knowledge and curriculum planning. Pupils should acquire some significant mastery of each of the forms, although there may be many different ways of designing a curriculum to achieve that end. Planning is particularly important for Hirst because he sees teaching essentially as a means-end activity. It is necessary first to plan the desired ends — the objectives — and then to plan effective means of teaching to arrive at those points. At this stage the model is all-important.

Curriculum Models

A curriculum model is not, however, simply an expression of a philosophical theory. It is also an incorporation of social and possibly economic ideas. There are at least two models which need to be examined at this stage: the behavioural objectives model and the cultural analysis approach to curriculum planning.

The behavioural objectives model

The objectives model[12] has a long history in the USA and also has something in common with the payment by results approach adopted in nineteenth-century England (see Chapter 1). From the first decade of the twentieth century educationists in the USA such as Franklin Bobbitt[13] attempted to apply the industrial techniques developed by F. W. ('Speedy') Taylor to educational environments. Detailed lists of objectives were drawn up and costed. Achievement of results by pupils was the only criterion of success. After some short-lived publicity this approach to educational planning faded into the background, but never disappeared completely, being pushed out of sight by the influence of Dewey and progressive attitudes to schools.

The objectives approach was given new credibility in the late 1940s by the work of Ralph Tyler. His book *Basic Principles of Curriculum and Instruction* (1949) was one of the foundation books in curriculum theory. Tyler suggested that there were four fundamental questions which must be answered in connection with any teaching programme:

1 What educational purposes should the school seek to attain?
2 What educational experiences can be provided that are likely to achieve these purposes?
3 How can these educational experiences be effectively organised?
4 How can we determine whether these purposes are being attained?

These four basic questions have been translated into the objectives model in the following way:

1 aims and objectives;
2 content;
3 organisation;
4 evaluation.

Tyler, like many other curriculum theorists, including Benjamin Bloom[14] a few years later, was encouraged to develop his model by the fact that many educational programmes were so ill-defined that they were incapable of evaluation — no teacher could ever know whether he was successful or not. But what began as a desire for clarity has often been transformed into a theory where the only valid educational objectives are those which describe pupil behaviour in measurable terms. The objectives model — and in its extreme form the behavioural objectives model — has flourished especially in the USA and was given an additional lease of life by such theoretical approaches as 'the taxonomy of educational objectives' by Benjamin Bloom and his colleagues in the 1950s.[15]

The essence of the behavioural objectives model is that the curriculum must be defined in terms of changes in pupils' behaviour which are pre-specified and measurable. This is an extremely narrow view of the teaching and learning process. Many critics would suggest that this is an appropriate model for training but not for education: it would be a useful model for teaching typewriting or even multiplication tables and some kinds of simple arithmetic, but not for philosophy, English Literature, or history. It is suggested that for education the emphasis must be on the input rather than on the output. For this reason the behavioural objectives model is often referred to as the output model or the industrial model, or the factory model. The implication here is, as I suggested earlier in this chapter, that the social influence which dominates this model is that of an advantaged group in industrial and capitalist society.

The objections to the model are practical as well as theoretical. Even if it were desirable it would be impossible to list all the behavioural objectives necessary in even one area of knowledge. In the social studies field, for example, some American curriculum planners attempted to produce a list of objectives in the social studies area, but abandoned the project when they had reached something like 4,000 detailed objectives.

It is perhaps necessary to emphasise the difference in approach between objectives and behavioural objectives. Philosophers such as Paul Hirst might claim to operate within an objectives model, or perhaps with an objectives approach, but not confine themselves to behavioural objectives. In the USA, however, the objectives model has become almost completely identified with behavioural objectives. This approach is also related to behaviourist psychology.[16]

The cultural analysis model

Some would claim that this model is also American in origin. It has sometimes been identified with Smith, Stanley and Shores (1957), and Broudy, Smith and Burnett (1964). They put forward a view of curriculum based on the idea of common culture and common curriculum. It might also be claimed, however, that this approach has a long history in the English context. Whenever anyone wishes to change the curriculum in England, there has been a tendency to justify this in terms of culture. This goes back at least as far as Matthew Arnold in the nineteenth century; more recently, in 1958 Raymond Williams produced his book *Culture and Society*, and in 1962, *The Long Revolution*, both of which have been influential. Williams went so far as to produce a model common curriculum based on the idea of common culture and what everyone needs to know in a democratic society.[17]

The Australian Malcolm Skilbeck, working in England, came to similar conclusions about educational and curriculum analysis. Skilbeck refers to his own scheme as situational analysis, although it seems to be much wider than that. According to Skilbeck, individual schools have to come to terms with the social context of the school and plan a curriculum accordingly. He suggests a sequence of stages:

1 situational analysis;
2 goal formulation;
3 programme building;
4 interpretation and implementation;
5 monitoring, feedback, assessment and reconstruction.

Some would suggest that this is not very different from an objectives model (provided that the objectives are not behavioural objectives) except that there is more emphasis on situational analysis which includes cultural analysis. Skilbeck breaks down situational analysis into external and internal. The external situational analysis includes:

1 Cultural and social changes, and expectations including parental expectations, employer requirements, community assumptions and values, changing relationships and ideology;
2 educational system requirements and challenges;
3 the changing nature of the subject matter;
4 the potential contribution of teachers' support systems;

5 the flow of resources into the school.

The internal situational analysis consists of:

1 Pupils; aptitudes, abilities and educational needs;
2 teachers: values, attitudes, skills, knowledge, experience, etc.;
3 school ethos and political structure;
4 material resources;
5 perceived and felt problems and shortcomings in the existing curriculum.

This is a very useful check list for those about to embark at a school level on the process of curriculum change, but much more work is necessary on the 'cultural and social changes and expectations' as well as 'the changing nature of the subject matter'.[18]

In the UK in recent years there has been a good deal of discussion about the curriculum and both of the above models have been implicitly involved.

The HMI document *Curiculum 11-16* (1976) was based on the idea of access to a common culture by means of a common curriculum. The arguments employed are very similar to those of curriculum theorists of the cultural analysis school. The 1980 DES document *A Framework for the School Curriculum* is based on the idea of a core curriculum, minimum competency, output rather than input, and testing. In this respect, the core curriculum and the 1980 *Framework* have much more in common with the Assessment of Performance Unit (APU)[19] set up by the DES in 1975, than the work by HMI on *Curriculum 11-16*. Officially, the APU has nothing to do with curriculum planning and APU officers have been careful to say that they do not want to influence the curriculum in any way. But any official test will tend to encourage teaching to the test and it is difficult to see how the APU can avoid 'backwash'. The APU being based on testing procedures has much more in common with the behavioural objectives approach than with cultural analysis. The APU is planned according to six kinds of development which will need to be broken down into test items. The model here is an output model whereas *Curriculum 11-16*, based on areas of experience, is much closer to an input model.

It might also be argued that in England examinations dominate the curriculum and play the most significant part in secondary education, including curriculum planning. They have become objectives rather than a means of evaluation.

Summary

Utopian ideas of curriculum planning are almost certainly doomed to failure, but that should not prevent us from trying to make curricula more rational and effective. Philosophical views of the structure of knowledge are contrasted with sociological concerns about social differences. Two curriculum planning models are examined: the behavioural objectives approach (a Utopian model?) and cultural analysis. Recent developments in the debate about the curriculum in England are examined in the light of these two models: it is suggested that the 1980 *Framework* and the APU approach are dangerously close to the mechanistic, behaviourist model and that we would be better advised to try to improve upon such documents as *Curriculum 11-16* in the cultural analysis tradition.

NOTES

1 **Curriculum planning** only becomes an issue, however, when there are proposals, perhaps conflicting proposals, to change educational policy in some way. At times of social and educational consensus there will be no controversy about the curriculum and therefore no need to discuss planning or morals.

2 **Some would suggest** that dispositions or attitudes towards education are more important than knowledge in a narrow sense — that is, that we all tend to forget so much knowledge in the long run that this may not be very important; on the other hand, attitudes acquired during the educational process are enduring. An interest in history and a critical attitude towards evidence are much more important than 'knowing the facts'. When referring to 'knowledge' in this chapter, I am using the term very widely to include the acquisition of knowledge-based attitudes or dispositions.

3 **These are valid differences** in approach, but it is a pity sociologists often tend to ignore the work done by philosophers in this field and then to get involved in subject matter which is outside their competence. *See* Lawton (1975) for a discussion of these issues.

4 **The trivium** comprised grammar, rhetoric and logic; the more advanced quadrivium comprised arithmetic, music, geometry and astronomy. The trivium and quadrivium together made up the seven liberal arts.

5 **C. P. Snow** (1905-80), Lord Snow of Leicester. A scientist and novelist as well as a politician, Snow read a paper on 'The Two

Cultures and the Scientific Revolution', the 1959 Rede Lecture at Cambridge, in which he criticised the educational system for producing scientists and arts graduates who could not communicate with each other: scientists who failed to read and 'humanists' who could not understand the second law of thermodynamics. The lecture caused a good deal of discussion and has been much quoted ever since, but it was no more than a revival of the nineteenth-century debate between scientists and humanists.

6 **Karl Mannheim** (1893-1947), a German sociologist, who sought refuge in England during the 1930s, taught at the London School of Economics and became the first Professor of Sociology of Education in the University of London Institute of Education.

7 *See* Richard Pring, 'Knowledge out of Control', *Education for Teaching* (Autum 1972).

8 **I am here using 'man-made' or God-given'** metaphorically to indicate a distinction between those disciplines which exist as social conventions or as necessary logical categories. For example, in my view there are 'real' differences between mathematics and poetry, but the difference between sociology and anthropology is conventional — the boundaries could be redrawn or abolished altogether without posing any logical problems, which is not the case with mathematics and poetry.

9 **It has to be stressed,** of course, that many real life issues and problems involve more than one discipline — for example, environmental pollution involves questions of science, politics and economics. It probably means that schools should be concerned with integrating these disciplines but only when pupils have an understanding of what the disciplines are.

10 *See* Schwab (1964).

11 **Paul Hirst's** 1965 paper 'Liberal Education and the Nature of Knowledge' is now reprinted in Hirst (1975). This volume also includes 'The Forms of Knowledge Revisited' as well as a number of other interesting papers.

12 **Behavioural objectives.** It is important to emphasize the difference between objectives and behavioural objectives. Those who wish to plan a curriculum by means of objectives may mean no more than that they wish to become a little clearer about what they are trying to teach. However, some critics of that view, especially in the USA, claim that this is far too vague, and the only objectives worth having are behavioural objectives — that is, objectives which are pre-specified in terms of measurable changes in pupil behaviour. This makes the objectives very precise, but far too narrow to apply to educational programmes.

13 **Franklin Bobbitt** was an educational administrator who wrote a number of books and articles which are now only of historical interest — for example, *The Curriculum* (1918) and *How to Make a Curriculum*

(1924) (Houghton Mifflin). F.W. ('Speedy') Taylor (1856-1915) was a famous, or notorious, industrial psychologist who developed the subject of 'scientific management'. The main motive was to increase the output of workers in factories. The approach today is seen as mechanistic and far from scientific when applied to industry; it is thought to have very little relevance indeed to management in education.

14 *The Taxonomy of Educational Objectives* (Bloom *et al.* 1956) Bloom and his colleagues were motivated by the lack of clarity regarding examination procedures. In 1948 there was a meeting in Boston of college examiners; these psychologists became more and more aware of the fact that there was a great deal of confusion regarding aims, objectives, methods and terminology. Their attempt to clarify objectives resulted in the famous *Taxonomy*.

15 *See* Stenhouse (1975) and Eisner (1969) for criticisms of the behavioural objectives model. Hugh Sockett has also shown how the behavioural objectives model trivialises the teaching of science: 'Behavioural Objectives', *London Educational Review,* Vol. 2, No. 3, Autumn 1973.

16 **Behaviourist psychology** or behaviourism seeks to discover regularities in human behaviour by examining that behaviour in the context of observable external events occurring in the inter-action of man with his environment. Behaviourists insist that behavioural changes can be explained adequately without reference to 'mind', 'spirit', or 'will'. The names most associated with this school were J. B. Watson and B. F. Skinner. According to Skinner, for instruction to succeed motivation must always be present. The pupil must be presented with a stimulus and make an appropriate response, which must be rewarded or reinforced. Skinner claims to base a whole theory of education as well as curriculum planning on this simplistic basis.

17 **Raymond Williams'** version of common curriculum is contained in *The Long Revolution:*

(a) extensive practice in the fundamental languages of English and mathematics;
(b) general knowledge of ourselves and our environment, taught at the secondary stage not as separate academic disciplines, but as general knowledge drawn from the disciplines which clarify at a higher stage, i.e.,
   (i) biology, psychology;
   (ii) social history, law and political institutions, sociology, descriptive economics, geography including actual industry and trade;
   (iii) physics and chemistry;
(c) history and criticism of literature, the visual arts, music, drama performance, landscape and architecture;
(d) extensive practice in democratic procedures, including meetings, negotiations, and the selection and conduct of leaders in

democratic organizations. Extensive practice in the use of libraries, newspapers and magazines, radio and television programmes, and other sources of information, opinion and influence;

(e) introduction to at least one other culture, including its language, history, geography, institutions and arts, to be given in part by visiting and exchange.

18 *See* Chapter 2 for a discussion of the cultural analysis approach to curriculum planning.

19 *See* Chapter 1, Note 17, (p. 25) for the history of the APU.

8 Teachers and Pupils

We are nearing the end of the book, and it is appropriate that we should come back to a central concern of education: the teacher/pupil relationship. It is difficult to see the child as the centre of the educational process (except in a very limited and obvious sense), but it is reasonable to suggest that the teacher's task is to help the developing child to relate in a more meaningful way to his environment. For this process to be successful, a good relationship is necessary.

The Teacher-Pupil relationship

To take an example, I am occasionally asked to express an opinion about the Open University,[1] and I find it extremely difficult to give a sensible answer without appearing to give a lecture. The problem is this: I think very highly indeed of the achievements of the Open University, and regard it as one of the major successes of post-war English education, but its success is of necessity limited. In terms of curriculum (that is, course planning and the preparation of materials) the Open University courses are (with a few notorious exceptions) eminently superior to what students are offered in most traditional universties. But what a student does not get at the Open University is the kind of personal tuition which is expected in traditional universities. Now for some adults this may not matter, so the Open University can be counted as a success. But the idea of trying to educate *children* by means of materials rather than teachers is not feasible. We generally work on the assumption that a teacher is necessary, not only to provide materials for children but to act as a mediator between the child and the materials as well as between the child and knowledge in other forms. To explain, to answer questions and to hold discussions with children is the expected role of a schoolteacher. As we have seen, however, the problem with the one teacher/thirty pupils classroom norm is that teachers have tended to adopt a style approaching the lecture, attempting to explain and discuss with the class as a whole, whereas pupils often need individual attention. What else can teachers do? In a class of thirty and during a lesson of three-quarters of an hour, each child would only get one and a half minutes of teacher time as an individual even if nothing else happened during that lesson.

Most educationists assume, therefore, that there is an important difference between children learning and adults learning. (Many would say that *some* kinds of learning for adults are very difficult without personal interaction, and the Open University recognises this by encouraging students to form 'self-help' groups where there is no tutor available.) An important skill for schoolteachers to learn is how to relate successfully with pupils. Such evidence as exists would seem to indicate that some attempts to solve this problem are more successful than others: some teachers are simply better at promoting good relations with their pupils than others. Furthermore, the evidence of the Rutter[2] study shows that the secondary pupils who make most progress are those who perceive the teacher as someone who is prepared to help them, and to whom they can go for academic advice. I stress academic advice because there are perhaps too many teachers who like to play the role of amateur psychologist, or psychiatrist. Most pupils do not want or need that kind of help (and if they do, teachers may not be the best people to provide it); what most pupils want most of the time is sympathetic help to overcome problems or difficulties in their school work.

This brings us back to another point about the role of the teacher. Teachers must have some 'subject' expertise to offer and must be able to offer it in an appropriae manner. Teachers must feel confident that they have something worthwhile to offer and be prepared to make demands on pupils that pupils would not make on themselves if the school and teachers did not exist. And teachers must present their 'offerings' in such a way that pupils can come back to them. This is partly a question of learning how to ask questions and how to reply, but it is also concerned with other inter-personal skills as well, and an attitude of openness on the part of the teacher. Teachers need not love all their pupils — they may not even like all of them — but they must respect all of them.[3] This is one of the rights of all pupils — the right to have respect from the teachers in authority over them.

This view of the role of the teacher, and of the pupil/teacher relationship, may appear to be in conflict with some modern progressive thoughts on education, especially primary education. It is often suggested that the role of the teacher is to be a kind of facilitator in the child's own self-educational process. I have already indicated my disagreement with that point of view, but it will now be necessary to look more closely at this kind of child-centered 'progressive' argument.

It is perhaps unfortunate that certain views of education have been labelled as progressive when they represent an extremely old-fashioned and unscientific view of the nature of developing children. The main assumption behind what I would prefer to call the 'naive progressive' point of view is that the child knows best what is good for him (educationally as well as physically) so that he should be allowed complete freedom to decide what activities to get involved in at any particular time. A comparison is often made by some progressive educationists between a child choosing food and having the power to choose educational activities. They may quote the well-known experiment which allowed children in early infancy to choose their own food from a wide range of choice, and then measured what had been taken; it was established that all children had chosen a well-balanced diet. Unfortunately, it is usually not pointed out that when the infants were offered the range of food, certain kinds of choices were not available, such as cakes and chocolates. But it is precisely the difficulty of making certain choices available to the children when other attractions of a less desirable nature are in conflict that makes the task of the teacher extremely difficult.

Much of the philosophy of this kind of progressive education derives from Rousseau (1712-78), or possibly from misinterpretations of his philosophy. Rousseau's philosophy can best be understood as a reaction against the harsh teaching methods of his time, demanding happiness for children during their childhood rather than seeing childhood as a preparation for life in a corrupt society. As such, it was a useful doctrine, but an incomplete view of how to plan an educational programme. Pestalozzi (1746-1827) can be viewed in much the same way, and also Froebel (1782-1852). All three shared the view that children were born in a state of total goodness. More recently, the Scottish teacher, A.S. Neill, has followed in this same tradition.

Since A.S. Neill[4] has been enormously influential and much praised by those who wish to adopt various of his practices, it may be useful to spend a little time on an evaluation of Neill's educational practices. Several ex-pupils have written about their experiences at Summerhill, but the most systematic account was given by Emmanuel Bernstein (1967 and 1968) who interviewed fifty ex-pupils. According to Bernstein, twenty-six of the fifty complained of the lack of academic opportunity, and the poor quality of teaching at Summerhill. The role of the teacher was, in fact, never made clear. Neill was an authority of a charismatic kind, but he appeared to object to assistant teachers sharing this kind of role, and since he had little respect for conventional learning, it was difficult to see what the purpose of the teacher in his school might be. Another generally sympathetic critic (Hemmings 1972) has written that it was sometimes suggested that teachers were there to 'stoke the boiler and darn the socks'. Other criticisms of the school by the pupils included the suggestion that the self-expression type of regime favoured the extroverted child, but was much less suitable for shy, sensitive introverts. Bernstein's research showed that there were complaints about lack of protection against bullies, insufficient help in academic studies, and the fact that pupils gave up too easily in the face of difficult work.

In view of this negative evidence and the almost total lack of any systematic educational theory in any of the books written by A.S. Neill, it is difficult to see why his approach has been so highly regarded and his books so widely read. One possible answer is that many adults, including teachers, look back on their school days with something less than enthusiasm. Schools for many pupils are still monotonous, routine places where they are 'bossed about by teachers' rather than places where they can learn something of value. One reaction against the prison view of the school is to suggest that children should be much more free and also should be in much greater control over their own learning activities. The extreme version of this doctrine is, as we have seen, that children should be left to control their own learning, and to learn by discovery rather than by being told or given information by a teacher. Part of the problem here is that there is some truth in this educational doctrine, although both Rousseau and Neill got it wrong. Rousseau and Neill rightly objected to empty verbalisation — education being a series of pieces of information passed on from a learned teacher to an ignorant child. But they over-reacted, and suggested that *everything* should be learnt by discovery and experience, rather than by being told the answers by teachers or by books. This kind of naive progressivism, often dressed up with various kinds of jargon as 'discovery learning', has been attacked in a variety of ways by both Bantock (1969) and Ausubel (1968).

Bantock, in the second of the Black Papers on education, was particularly anxious to demolish the idea that children could discover everything for themselves. Bantock criticised those teachers who followed blindly Rousseau's command 'give your scholar no verbal lessons; he should be taught by experience alone'. Bantock pointed out that Rousseau seriously underestimated the power of language in education; Rousseau mistakenly believed that words always had something to which they referred, and that unless the thing to which the word referred had been experienced they simply constituted meaningless noises to children. In view of the amount of work that is being carried out on language development, it is now clear that Rousseau's view was incredibly naive. Bantock also suggests that children are capable of getting considerable joy out of uses of words which they cannot understand in the full sense. In some respects, children can only make discoveries for themselves when they have the necessary language to put their learning into some kind of meaningful framework. Bantock also criticised the progressive discovery method as leading to a 'magpie' curriculum, and a structureless context for learning.

Ausubel (1968) concentrates on the psychological misunderstanding present in the discovery approach. Ausubel is not completely opposed to discovery learning, but only to the dogma which suggests that discovery learning is the *only* appropriate method or is equally applicable to *all* forms of learning. In particular, Ausubel wanted to demolish what he referred to as 'a sentimental type of Rousseauean mysticism and primitivism'. Ausubel accepts some discovery methods as appropriate to the earlier stages of education, particularly when children have not passed beyond the concrete operational stage of cognitive development. Even at this stage, however, he suggests that learning by discovery should be in the context of guided discovery, but as a child's language develops, as he proceeds into Piaget's formal stage and learning becomes more abstract, then discovery methods become less and less applicable. Ausubel also makes the point that even where discovery learning may be appropriate it may not be 'cost-effective'. There is simply too much to be discovered, so the skilful teacher knows how much to allow children to discover for themselves, how much guidance to give, and where to step in with knowledge, information and instruction.

In view of the widely-held opinion, especially in primary schools, that discovery learning is the best approach, it may be useful to conclude with Ausubel's own summary. He suggests that first, most of the articles cited in the literature report no research findings; second, that most of the well-controlled studies report negative findings; third, that most studies reporting positive findings either fail to control other significant variables, or employ questionable techniques of statistical analysis. Ausubel's conclusion is that if we rely on research evidence, we would be extremely critical of the discovery learning approach. Ausubel winds up his argument by quoting from Stanley (1949), a passage which is so relevant in this context that I would like to reproduce it here:

> The infant is born into a logically ordered world, abounding in problem solutions accumulated during the long span of mankind's sojourn on earth and this distilled wisdom, called 'culture', constitutes his chief heritage. Were it wiped away, he would become, in all respects, a wild animal, even less well equipped to cope with nature than are the instinct-aided beasts of the jungle. An individual is sagacious in direct proportion to the facility with which he can acquire and use existing knowledge; for even the most brilliantly endowed person can make but few valuable original discoveries.
>
> (Stanley 1949, quoted by Ausubel 1968)

To submit children to this kind of 'discovery' curriculum may seem to be kind and even to promote liberty, but it is in fact in conflict with one of the major rights of children, namely, to have adequate access to knowledge and experience, or in Stanley's term, 'culture'.

Rights

The concept of rights is, however, by no means a simple one. Some would deny the word any philosophical validity; others emphasise the right of freedom; others the priority of the right of justice or fairness. If we are discussing the rights of pupils in schools, then one major point dominates this analysis. Any system of compulsory education is inevitably an infringement of the right of liberty, including the right to be free to decide for oneself whether to go to school or not, or whether to send one's children to school or not. Compulsory schooling is usually justified on two counts: first, that education is a self-evident benefit to children and this overrides the supposed wishes of those who are too young to make a rational decision. Second, some children will need to be protected against their own parents who might otherwise deprive them of the benefit of schooling for their own selfish motives. If the view is taken that compulsory schooling is justifiable, it then becomes necessary to be quite sure that the 'self-evident' value of education can in practice be spelt out. If young people are deprived of ten or eleven years of liberty, then the supposed advantages of schooling need to be put into the balance and therefore to be made explicit. These advantages of schooling may be expressed in terms of rights: we are then led on to the question of what rights should pupils be guaranteed in return for their loss of liberty.

I have already referred indirectly to some of these rights, but it may now be useful to set them out in a list and make some additions to the list. I would suggest, then, that all pupils who are compelled to attend school should be regarded as having the following rights:

1 to have the respect of their teachers;
2 to have a worthwhile curriculum;
3 not to have their time wasted unnecessarily;
4 to be treated fairly;
5 to be a member of a community or organisation with an adequate rule system;
6 to complain;
7 to choose some activities;
8 to participate in some aspects of decision-making.

1 Respect of teachers

As with many rights this right would be extremely difficult to define or to enforce, but it would be useful to establish it as a principle and hope that it might affect the attitudes of both teachers and pupils, as well as parents. Later, we shall be discussing the question of teachers' authority, but it is also important to establish that because teachers are in authority this does not entitle them to treat pupils as though they were inferior beings without the right of respect.

2 A worthwhile curriculum

This is related to the argument for a common curriculum discussed in earlier chapters. It is difficult to see how so much loss of liberty could be justified unless much more specific attention is given to spelling out the supposed advantages in terms of knowledge and experience. Also implied in this principle is the idea that every attempt should be made not only to satisfy the teachers and parents that there is a worthwhile curriculum which should be made available to the children, but also to explain it as worthwhile to the children themselves. (This is extremely difficult, especially for young children, but every attempt should be made.)

3 Profitable use of time

One of the most dispiriting aspects of many schools is the amount of time which is wasted. Some of this is an organisational problem, but teachers also have a responsibility to be sufficiently well organised to avoid wasting pupils' time. The fact that so much time is wasted and that this aspect of the school organisation is taken for granted is probably an indication that schools are still, in some respects, regarded as custodial institutions rather than educational ones. A visitor to many schools cannot help being struck by the fact that so much of the activity appears to be 'containment', or using up time rather than profitably making use of it.

4 The right to be treated fairly

Many social philosophers would suggest that the right to justice is the most basic of all rights. This is often recognised by children themselves who object very strongly to favouritism. Unfortunately, favouritism in many guises is still an aspect of schools and classrooms. Children are treated in a way which is often arbitrary and often clearly unjustifiable. For example, the idea of keeping in the whole class in order to punish one or two children cannot be justified in terms of justice, or of fairness.

5 An adequate rule system

I have commented elsewhere in this book on the fact that schools are sometimes organisd as it they were voluntary associations when they are compulsory establishments. There is often a desire to avoid any rule system. But the result of this is not greater freedom but greater arbitrariness, and sometimes chaos. A child who is compelled to be a member of a community such as a school has a right to expect that the school will be orderly, and that he will be protected from bullying either from other children or from members of staff. The rule system needs not only to exist, but also to be made available to all members of the community.

6 The right to complain

Again, it is perhaps a hangover from the school as a custodial institution that the child who complains is often regarded as a criminal for that in itself. I would go further and suggest that it is one of the duties of the school to teach children *how* to complain. There are ways of complaining which are offensive, and there are others which are not only much more effective, but which are much more acceptable to those in authority. This does not come naturally to children: they have to be taught. But the most important principle involved is that members of a community — especially a compulsory community where liberty is restricted — have the right to complain about the way in which they are treated, the quality of the curriculum and so on.

7 The right to choose

This is an extremely difficult right to discuss because it is a limited right. I have already argued that it would be reasonable to compel children to go to school and also to make certain aspects of the curriculum common or compulsory in that limited sense. It would be unreasonable, however, if children had *no* right of choice within the curriculum at all. There can be choice and should be choice outside the compulsory curriculum, and it is highly desirable that children learn to make choices relating to 'leisure' time or 'option' time. It would also be sensible to have a certain amount of choice within the common curriculum. This cannot involve giving up important aspects of knowledge, but it could involve, say, choosing one period of history rather than another.

8 Participation in decision-making

This is another difficult right to discuss because it is also a limited right. In one sense, of course, pupils participate even in the most authoritarian and oppressive school environment — unless they participate they will not be educated at all, since no one can be educated without some kind of participation. A further distinction needs to be made between those kinds of activities and decision-making in which participation by pupils is appropriate, and those in which pupils have no right to participate. If we regard education as a process of initiating pupils into various kinds of knowledge, then there must be teachers who are in possession of the knowledge which is to be passed on. Pupils are not in possession of that knowledge, or at least not to the same extent as the teachers (if they were, the teachers would unnecessary). It is in this sense that teachers must be regarded as authorities on what they teach.

It is also important to point out that teachers are not absolute authorities, but they must be authorities relative to the pupils. It is one of the difficulties of the teacher's role to encourage pupils to ask questions and even to argue against the point of view put by a teacher, yet to do so without yielding the authority position entirely.

In most aspects concerning what is taught, therefore, the decision-making must be that of the teacher. Teachers alone are authorities in this respect. Pupils might make suggestions about what would be more interesting within the subject matter being offered, but ultimately it must be the teacher who decides whether something is essential or optional. On the other hand, in so far as school decisions affect pupils as members of an organisation, and even as learners within that organisation, they have a right to be heard, since they are, in a limited sense, authorities as pupils. Pupil participation in decision-making would be entirely appropriate in that area although it does not necessarily result in a 'one man, one vote' situation. The schools can become more democratic, but cannot be democracies in the full sense of that word.

On the other hand there are certain rights which pupils do not have and should not expect. This includes the fact that pupils do not have a right to expect to be entertained, to be allowed to follow their own interests all the time, to reject everything that is offered by teachers, to disregard the rightful authority of teachers, to ignore the rules of the institution, and so on. If all of this were made explicit it would be possible to arrive at a kind of school social contract in which rights and responsibilities were balanced. This is often assumed in schools, but rarely made explicit to the pupils. If such a code were made explicit, it would then make the classroom teacher's task of fostering good relations with pupils much easier.

Rights of Teachers

We should not lose sight of the notion that teachers also have rights. They have the right to expect attention and respect from their students and the right to exercise the authority which is a necessary part of a teacher's role. In a system of democratic accountability, teachers also have a right to information from, and consultation by, their 'superiors' in the educational system — for example, headteachers, governors and LEA officials.

Conclusion

From the 1944 Education Act to the end of the 1950s, education was generally regarded in a spirit of optimism. It was taken for granted that education was 'a good thing', benefitting individuals and the country at large. Money was spent generously, if not lavishly, on new school buildings, large numbers of teachers were trained, curriculum development of various kinds was undertaken. The provision of places in universities was greatly expanded, partly as an economic investment and partly to satisfy the increasing demand for higher education.

By the 1960s, however, the tide was beginning to turn. Disillusionment with education was setting in. Reference has already been made to the Black Papers, beginning in 1969, which encapsulated a good deal of public opinion about education in the 1960s. These Papers (some, but not all, ill-formed and badly written) complained about lower standards, sloppy teaching methods and a general drift away from traditional qualities in education. Primary schools were suspected of being too little concerned with basic skills; comprehensive schools and the raising of the school leaving age had not produced a magic solution to 'secondary education for all', and occasionally, the press delighted in presenting stories of schools where discipline had broken down. During the 1970s this disaffection was combined with a deteriorating economic situation which produced calls for 'value for money' and accountability. At the same time, there were critics from within the educational fold as well as outside. The deschoolers suggested that compulsory schooling did more harm than good; some sociologists of education made equally radical attacks on education as an institution. Their intention was to make schools better places for pupils and teachers by questioning traditions and existing institutions, but the general result was to depress the morale of teachers and to add ammunition to those right-wing critics of education who wanted both a return to older systems combined with a smaller expenditure.

The result has been an increased demand for accountability in schools. This in itself might be no bad thing, but it will all depend on the kind of accountability which is invoked. Let us examine the two extreme possibilities: if accountability simply means that teachers will be expected to explain, to parents and pupils in particular, what they are doing and why, with special attention to developing ways of evaluating successes and failures within the classroom, then accountability in general must be a considerable benefit. If, on the other hand, accountability means a greater emphasis on objective tests and concern for standards in a narrow sense, then the result is likely to be what has been related elsewhere[5] in this book — the behavioural objectives model, with consequent dehumanisation of schools, deterioration of pupil/teacher relations, a narrowing of the curriculum, too much concern with short-term results at the expense of long-term benefits; indications of output rather than concern for the quality of input. Those advocating, or even acquiescing to, that kind of accountability should look carefully at recent experience in the USA where education has been trivialised in the cause of testing and accountability.

If that kind of accountability can be avoided, however, and educationists can move in the direction of a more open system of schooling, then a good deal of what has preceded this chapter in this book will be relevant. Schools will be more concerned with techniques of self-evaluation and self-improvement; teachers' interpersonal skills will be at a premium. Higher standards will be expected, but not an obsessive concern with objective tests and measurement. All that will require better teachers. If teachers are to possess this kind of professional autonomy, then they will need to develop professional skills and adequate knowledge: they will need to be able to plan and evaluate syllabuses and teaching schemes; they will need to be able to build-in a variety of approaches to difficult topics, and a variety of teaching methods. They will be experts at record-keeping as well as good classroom practitioners. In short, they will be experts in teaching and learning.

NOTES

1 **The Open University.** The idea was first made public by Harold Wilson in 1963, and in 1966 there was a Government White Paper on the idea of 'A University of the Air'. A Planning Committee was established, chaired by Sir Peter Venables. The report of this Committee was accepted and the Open University received a Charter as an independent degree-awarding institution. The first students were enrolled in 1970. By 1973, there were over 40,000 students enrolled. The Open University receives funds by direct grant from the DES (unlike other universities which are funded via the University Grants Committee). A major feature of the Open University is that no formal entry requirements are called for. It is intended to give a second chance to mature adults who for some reason either failed to get the necessary GCE O-levels and A-levels at school, or who did not proceed to university at the usual age of eighteen or nineteen. Degrees are awarded on a credit system, so that there is no formal time limit involved. Students can do one or two units a year and miss a year occasionally if they wish to. Six credits will give a student an Ordinary degree, eight are needed for an Honours degree. No attendance is required at a university, but some courses involve short residential summer schools. Clearly, the burden of learning is on the student rather than on the tutors, although some provision for tutorial assistance is made. In general, students work very largely on their own with materials sent through the post combined with radio and television programmes.

2 **Rutter** *et al.* (1979); see Chapter 4, Note 13, p. 80.

3 **Some teachers** may feel that if they are required to display respect for pupils this will weaken their authority. This need not be the case: there is no contradiction between giving respect and being seen as in authority. In fact, a rational, bureaucratic (in the sense discussed earlier) approach to authority would stress the need for authority-receiving to be accompanied by respect-giving. Without that balance, we would be getting dangerously close to authoritarianism.

4 **A.S. Neill** (1883-1973), born in Forfar, near Dundee, Scotland where his father was a school master. Neill attended his father's school until the age of fourteen. He was not a successful pupil. After two years' work Neill became an apprentice school master, but failed, after four years, to qualify for further training. After some uncertificated teaching he matriculated and eventually obtained a degree at Edinburgh University. He then taught for twelve years in Scottish schools. After the 1914-18 War, Neill drifted into 'progressive' education in England and then in Germany, where he met Frau Neustatter, whom he later married. They returned to England and founded Summerhill School, at first in Dorset, transferring to Suffolk in 1927, where Neill remained until his death. Neill wrote a large number of books about his educational 'philosophy' and practice, from *A Dominie's Log* (1915) to *Talking of Summerhill* (1967).

5 *See* Chapter 7 on the dangers of the behavioural objectives approach.

BIBLIOGRAPHY

ARNOLD, M. (1869) *Culture and Anarchy*. Cambridge: Cambridge University Press.

AUSUBEL, D. P. (1968) *Psychology: A Cognitive View*. New York: Holt, Rinehart and Winston.

BANKS, O. (1955) *Parity and Prestige in English Secondary Education*. London: Routledge and Kegan Paul.

BANTOCK, G. H. (1969) 'Discovery methods', in COX, C. B. and DYSON, A. E. (eds) *Black Paper Two: The Crisis in Education*. London: Critical Quarterly Society.

BANTOCK, G. H. (1975) 'Towards a theory of popular education', in GOLBY, M., *et al. Curriculum Design*. London: Croom Helm.

BARKER, R. (1972) *Education and Politics*. Oxford: Oxford University Press.

BARKER, R. G. and GUMP, P. V. (1964) *Big School, Small School: High School Size and Student Behaviour*. Stanford, Calif.: Stanford University Press.

BARNES, D., BRITTON, J. and ROSEN, H. (1969) *Language, the Learner and the School*. Harmondsworth: Penguin Books.

BENN, C. and SIMON, B. (1970) *Half Way There*. New York and Maidenhead: McGraw Hill.

BENNETT, N. (ed.) (1976) *Teaching Styles and Pupil Progress*. Shepton Mallet: Open Books.

BERNSTEIN, E. (1968) 'What does a Summerhill old school tie look like?', *Psychology Today*, October 1968 (pp. 38-41, 70).

BIERSTEDT, R. (1967) 'The problem of authority', in ROSE, P. (ed.) *The Study of Society*. New York: Random House.

BLOOM, B. S. *et al.* (1956) *Taxonomy of Educational Objectives. Handbook I, The Cognitive Domain*. London: Longmans.

BLOOM, B. S. (1971) 'Mastery learning and its implications for curriculum development', in EISNER, E. (ed.) *Confronting Curriculum Reform*. Boston, Mass.: Little, Brown.

BOARD OF EDUCATION (1938) *Report of the Consultative Committee on Secondary Education* (The Spens Report). London: H. M. S. O.

BROUDY, H.S., SMITH, B.O. and BURNETT, J.R. (1964) *Democracy and Excellence in American Secondary Education*. Chicago, Ill.: Rand McNally.

BRUNER, J. (1960) *The Process of Education*. Cambridge, Mass: Harvard University Press.

BRUNER, J. (1966) *Toward a Theory of Instruction*. Cambridge, Mass.: Harvard University Press.

CARROLL, J. B. (1963) 'A model of school learning', *Teachers College Record*, Vol. 64.

CENTRAL ADVISORY COUNCIL FOR EDUCATION (1954) *Early Leaving*. London: H. M. S. O.

CENTRAL ADVISORY COUNCIL FOR EDUCATION (1963) *Children and their Primary Schools*. (The Plowden Report). London: H. M. S. O.

DENT, H. C. (1977) *Education in England and Wales*. London: Hodder and Stoughton.

DEPARTMENT OF EDUCATION AND SCIENCE (1977) *A New Partnership for our Schools* (The Taylor Report). London: H. M. S. O.

DEPARTMENT OF EDUCATION AND SCIENCE (1978) *Primary Education in England*. London: H. M. S. O.

DEPARTMENT OF EDUCATION AND SCIENCE (1979) *Aspects of Secondary Education in England* (The Secondary School Survey). London: H. M. S. O.

DEPARTMENT OF EDUCATION AND SCIENCE (1980) *A View of the Curriculum*. London H.M.S.O.

DEPARTMENT OF EDUCATION AND SCIENCE (1977) *Curriculum 11-16*. London: H. M. S. O.

DEPARTMENT OF EDUCATION AND SCIENCE (1977) *Education in Schools: A Consultative Document* (Green Paper). London: H. M. S. O.

EISNER, E. (1969) 'Instructional and expressive educational objectives', in POPHAM, W. J. *et al.* (eds) *Instructional Objectives*. Chicago, Ill.: Rand McNally.

EVANS, K. (1975) *The Development and Structure of the English Educational System*. London: Hodder and Stoughton.

FORD, J. (1969) *Social Class and the Comprehensive School*. London: Routledge and Kegan Paul.

GOODMAN, P. (1962) *Compulsory Miseducation*. New York: Horizon Press; Harmondsworth: Penguin Books (1971)

GORDON, P. and LAWTON, D. (1978) *Curriculum Change in the Nineteenth and Twentieth Centuries*. London: Hodder and Stoughton.

HANNAM, C., SMYTH, P. and STEPHENSON, N. (1971) *Young Teachers and Reluctant Learners*. Harmondsworth: Penguin Books.

HEMMINGS, N. (1972) *Fifty Years of Freedom*. London: Allen and Unwin.

HIRST, P. H. (1975) *Knowledge and Curriculum*. London: Routledge and Kegan Paul.

HOLT, J. (1964) *How Children Fail*. New York: Pitman Publishing; Harmondsworth: Penguin Books (1969).

HOLT, J. (1972) *Freedom and Beyond*. New York: Dutton; Harmondsworth: Penguin Books (1973).

HURMAN, A. (1979) *A Charter for Choice*. Windsor: National Foundation for Educational Research.

ILLICH, I. (1971) *Deschooling Society*. New York: Harper and Row; London: Calder and Boyars.

JEFFCOATE, R. (1977) 'Curriculum planning in multi-racial education'. *Educational Research*, Vol. 18, No. 3.

KOGAN, M. (1978) *The Politics of Educational Change*. Manchester: Manchester University Press.

KOHLBERG, L. (1964) 'Development of moral character and moral ideology', in HOFFMAN, M. L. and HOFFMAN, L. W. (eds) *Review of Child Development Research*, Vol. 1. Beverly Hills, Calif.: Sage.

LAWTON, D. (1975) *Class, Culture and the Curriculum*. London: Routledge and Kegan Paul.

LAWTON, D. (1977) *Education and Social Justice*. Beverly Hills, Calif.: Sage.

LAWTON, D. (1980) *The Politics of the School Curriculum*. London: Routledge and Kegan Paul.

MacRAE, D. (1961) *Ideology and Society*. London: Heinemann.

MAY, P. R. (1971) *Moral Education in Schools*. London: Methuen.

MOORE, T. W. (1974) *Educational Theory: An introduction*. London: Routledge and Kegan Paul.

PARKINSON, M. (1970) *The Labour Party and the Organisation of Secondary Education 1918-65*. London: Routledge and Kegan Paul.

PEEL, E. A. (1968) *The Pupil's Thinking*. London: Oldbourne.

PEEL, E. A. (1971) *The Nature of Adolescent Judgement*. London: Staples.

PETERS, R. S. (1966) *Ethics and Education*. London: Allen and Unwin.

PETERS, R. S. (ed.) (1968) *Perspectives on Plowden*. London: Routledge and Kegan Paul.

POPPER, K. R. (1966) *The Open Society and its Enemies*. London: Routledge and Kegan Paul.

PRING, R. (1972) 'Knowledge out of control'. *Education for Teaching*, Autumn.

RAISON, T. (1976) *The Act and the Partnership*. London: Centre for Studies in Social Policy.

RAWLS, J. (1972) *A Theory of Justice*. Oxford: Oxford University Press.

ROBERTSON, J. (1981) *Effective Classroom Control*. London: Hodder and Stoughton.

RUSSELL, B. (1946) *History of Western Philosophy* (Unwin University Books). London: Allen and Unwin.

RUTTER, M. *et al.* (1979) *Fifteen Thousand Hours: Secondary schools and their effects on children*. Shepton Mallet: Open Books.

SCHWAB, J. J. (1964) 'Structure of the disciplines: meaning and significances', in FORD, G. W. and PUGNO, L. (eds) *The Structure of Knowledge and the Curriculum*. Chicago, Ill.: Rand McNally.

SIMON, B. (1971) *Intelligence, Psychology and Education*. London: Lawrence and Wishart.

SMITH, B. O., STANLEY, W. O. and SHORES, J. H. (1957) *Fundamentals of Curriculum Development*. New York: Harcourt Brace and World.

STENHOUSE, L. (1975) *An Introduction to Curriculum Research and Development*. London: Heinemann.

STONE, M. (1978) *Black Culture, Self Concept and Schooling*. Unpublished Ph. D. thesis, University of Surrey.

TOUGH, J. (1973) *Focus on Meaning: Talking to some purpose with young children*. London: Allen and Unwin.

TYLER, R. W. (1949) *Basic Principles of Curriculum and Instruction*. Chicago, Ill.: University of Chicago Press.

VERNON, P.E. (ed.) (1957) *Secondary School Selection*. London: Methuen.

WHITE, J. (1975) 'The end of the compulsory curriculum', in *The Curriculum* (Studies in Education 2). London: University of London Institute of Education.

WILLIAMS, R. (1958, 1971) *Culture and Society*. Harmondsworth: Penguin Books.

WILLIAMS, R. (1961) *The Long Revolution*. Harmondsworth: Penguin Books.

INDEX